Praise for
THE CONSERVATIVE CASE FOR TRUMP

"Phyllis Schlafly is an American treasure who has been fighting the good fight for American sovereignty and cultural renewal for five decades. Without Phyllis, there'd be no Donald Trump. This book by Phyllis Schlafly, Ed Martin, and Brett Decker shows why Republicans not supporting Trump are helping elect Hillary Clinton."

—LAURA INGRAHAM, radio host and editor of LifeZette

"Donald Trump has dominated the election conversation in the 2016 cycle for a reason: he strikes a chord with voters who are sick of a political class that is running America into the ground. In *The Conservative Case for Trump*, Phyllis Schlafly, Ed Martin and Brett M. Decker show how President Trump can get our country back on the right track, and why Republicans and independents need to unify behind his candidacy."

—NEWT GINGRICH, former Speaker of the House

"Phyllis Schlafly has been a brave, badly needed voice of resistance to the takeover of the Republican Party by business interests and bloodless ideologues who'd love to flood America with cheap immigrant workers (to do the jobs they haven't already outsourced to other nations). Early on, she recognized the potential for Donald Trump to rebuild her party along more patriotic, common sense—and, she would say, Reaganesque—lines. What comes through in these pages by Schlafly, Martin, and Decker is the calm reason of veteran Republicans and patriots who can't be bought or intimidated. I think a lot of Democratic patriots will be persuaded too."

—MICKEY KAUS, journalist and author

"*The Conservative Case for Trump* is nothing less than the case for saving America from socialist tyranny cemented into place with the votes of millions of Third-World immigrants. It is the case for making a U-turn to expand economic opportunity, an America First foreign policy, preserving our constitutional rights—especially our First and Second Amendment rights—and ending the insanity of government-enforced political correctness. Every conservative needs to read this book and heed the wisdom of the heroic Phyllis Schlafly."

—DR. THOMAS DILORENZO, professor of economics,
Loyola University Maryland; senior faculty, Ludwig von Mises Institute; and author of *The Problem with Socialism*

The CONSERVATIVE CASE for
TRUMP

PHYLLIS SCHLAFLY
ED MARTIN
BRETT M. DECKER

REGNERY
PUBLISHING
A Division of Salem Media Group

Regnery® is a registered trademark of Salem Communications Holding Corporation

Cataloging-in-Publication Data on file with the Library of Congress

ISBN 978-1-62157-628-0

Published in the United States by
Regnery Publishing
A Division of Salem Media Group
300 New Jersey Ave NW
Washington, DC 20001
www.Regnery.com

Manufactured in the United States of America

10 9 8 7 6 5 4 3 2 1

Books are available in quantity for promotional or premium use. For information on discounts and terms, please visit our website: www.Regnery.com.

Distributed to the trade by
Perseus Distribution
250 West 57th Street
New York, NY 10107

Dedicated to our families and their future

CONTENTS

10

Introduction

I'm saddened by what I see happening to our country.
We're being humiliated, disrespected, and badly abused.
Obama was a leftist experiment that has failed. We cannot
afford four more years of this mess.

—Donald J. Trump

The revolution to take back America starts now. Donald Trump might seem an unlikely candidate to some, but he offers the American public something it's been yearning for: "a choice, not an echo"; a candidate not intimidated by political correctness or the liberal media. Donald Trump is our choice for president not only because he can win—I remember Everett Dirksen's famous speech at the 1952 Republican Convention when he publicly taunted the kingmakers: "We followed you before and you led us down the path to defeat"—but also because when you examine what he says and believes you discover an American patriot with policies that will make America great again.

I know that some well-meaning conservatives find Trump puzzling or even offensive, but I trust that this book—the culmination, for me, of more than seventy years of active involvement in Republican politics— might help sway them. My coauthor Ed Martin brings his own expertise in politics particularly in Missouri, as a former chief of staff to a Republican governor and as a former chairman of the Missouri Republican Party. My other coauthor Brett Decker is an expert on foreign policy and trade, having worked for the *Wall Street Journal* in Hong Kong and at the Export-Import Bank, and as a conservative opinion-maker as the former editorial page editor of the *Washington Times*.

We believe that not only can Donald Trump beat Hillary Clinton in the general election, but that he could be the most conservative president we've had since Ronald Reagan.

The stakes are unmistakably high. President Obama's effort to fundamentally transform America is on the brink of success—despite our having elected Republican majorities in both houses of Congress. The GOP has proven ineffectual at stopping Obama, who has thrown open the gates to illegal immigrants; emasculated our military; ruled by decree through presidential orders; waged the most extensive and extreme culture war in American history to the point of dictating to the nation that men should be allowed into women's changing rooms, restrooms, and locker rooms; exploded the national debt to an eye-popping $20 trillion; and built a legacy of foreign policy disasters from the rise of ISIS and the chaos of Libya and Syria to an emboldened China and Iran.

What will Hillary Clinton do if elected president? She will take Obama's transformation of America to the next level.

Here is what Hillary has pledged to do:[1]

- **On Immigration, continue Obama's flouting of our nation's laws:** "If Congress won't act, I'll defend President Obama's executive actions—and *I'll go even further*," she says, flooding the country with even more immigrants, all on a fast-track to citizenship.
- **On Guns, executive orders that could threaten our Second Amendment rights:** "If Congress refuses to act to end the epidemic of gun violence, I'll take administrative action to do so," Clinton has tweeted.

- **On Obamacare, more mandates:** "I'll defend the Affordable Care Act, build on its successes, and *go even further*," including "more options for undocumented people to be able to get the health care they need."
- **On Energy, more "green" regulation:** "I don't think we need to have a pipeline bringing dirty oil, exploiting the tar sands in western Canada across our border," Hillary said about the Keystone XL pipeline.[2] Clinton also promised that her administration would "put a lot of coal miners and coal companies out of business."[3]
- **On Abortion, more government-funding for Planned Parenthood, America's biggest abortion mill:** "As president, I'll stand up for Planned Parenthood and women's access to critical health services, including safe, legal abortion."
- **On Gay "Marriage," it's just the beginning:** "The U.S. Supreme Court's ruling on marriage equality represents America at its best: just, fair, and moving toward equality. *Now we have more work to do.* I'll fight to ensure that

lesbian, gay, bisexual, and transgender Americans have full equality under the law, and to end discrimination in employment, housing, schools, and other aspects of society."

- **On Foreign Policy, more global chaos:** If you liked President Obama's foreign policy, you'll love Hillary Clinton's version that brought us, when she was secretary of State, the failed "reset" of relations with Russia, lying to the American people (Benghazi), leading from behind (Libya), meaningless red lines (Syria), and a world in which American power has rapidly diminished.

This is what Hillary stands for, and with the power of executive appointments, the federal bureaucracy and the federal judiciary would be crammed full of Obama-Clinton clones, all eager to advance the growth of the federal government, stamp out traditional values, and promote crony capitalism where the federal government grants subsidies to favored businesses and strangles others with endless bureaucratic regulation.

Donald Trump's agenda is entirely different. He knows what is at stake and has promised to reverse

America's decline under Obama and make America great again; and he has shown far more fight on at least five major issues than the Republican Congress has—issues that resonate with the American people. For instance:

- **On Immigration:** Trump has made clear that the flood of illegal aliens crossing the border has to be stopped as a matter of national security, respect for the law, and putting the interests of Americans first—including American safety from foreign drug gangs, potential terrorists, and released illegal immigrant felons; and also the interests of American workers, a record number of whom are out of work because of cheap foreign labor.
- **On Trade:** Barack Obama believes in "free trade." So does Hillary Clinton. So do many Republicans. "Free trade" is not necessarily a "conservative" issue given that so many liberal Democrats are in favor it; and they favor it not just on grounds of economic efficiency but because they believe free trade and globalism bring peace and prosperity to

poorer nations, a theory that hasn't always proved out in practice. Conservatives, however, want trade deals that serve America's national interests—the interests not just of corporate bosses, or of liberal globalists who don't put America first, but the interests of American workers and American security. Donald Trump thinks that all too often the people who negotiate our free trade agreements do so without regard to America's national interests—and he's right. "Free trade" as it exists today isn't "free" at all and it certainly isn't fair, at least to the United States. Over the last twenty-five years, the United States has had a global trade deficit with 101 countries amounting to $12 *trillion*.[4] Our lopsided commerce with the Communist People's Republic of China, hardly a haven of freedom or free trade, has totaled $4 trillion over the last twenty-five years, and accounts for 60 percent of the U.S. trade deficit all on its own. The global trade deficit has cost the United States more than 6 million jobs, chiefly at the expense of

America's industrial heartland.[5] Donald Trump says that trade deals need to put American workers, America's industrial base, and our national security interests ahead of unthinking ideological commitment to a free trade system where only we play by the "free trade" rules. He's absolutely right.

- **On Islamism:** Global jihad waged by fanatical Muslims poses a clear and present danger to the national security of the United States. President Obama has notoriously banned the American government from naming our enemy. He has made it a priority to appease radical groups like the Muslim Brotherhood. And he has rolled out the welcome mat to Islamic "refugees" and immigrants. Hillary Clinton promises more of the same failed policies and proposes that the United States should import tens of thousands more unvetted Muslims from jihad-torn Syria.[6] Trump says the safety of Americans should come first. He is not afraid to name our enemy. He believes in containing the Islamist threat. And he believes that because our government is incompetent at vetting the backgrounds of Muslim immigrants, we should have a moratorium on immigrants from at least certain Muslim countries until we can be sure that we are not importing terrorists who might threaten the safety of our people. Restricting immigration in the interests of national security is a power that the courts have repeatedly held is well within the constitutional realm of the president.[7] Here as elsewhere, President Trump would put American interests first.

- **On Foreign Policy:** Donald Trump has rightly pointed out that the United States should not be in the business of "nation-building," that we should fight wars only when necessary to defend our national interests, and that we should encourage our NATO allies and other countries to do more to defend themselves. Like Ronald Reagan, Donald Trump believes in peace through strength. He would rebuild our military for the very purpose of *deterring* aggression. It's not "conservative" to fight endless wars abroad. Our foreign policy orthodoxies, Republican and Democrat, have long been in need of a re-think, and Donald Trump is providing it.

- **On Social Security:** Trump thinks Social Security can be saved without cutting benefits or raising the qualifying age for recipients.[8] As Trump explains, "Social Security is here to stay. To be sure, we must reform it, root out the fraud, make it more efficient, and ensure that the program is solvent. People have lived up to their end of the bargain and paid into the program in good faith. Of course they believe they're 'entitled' to receive the benefits they paid for—they are!"[9] Libertarians might not agree with Trump on this, but most Americans do and it is a conservative position.

On issue after issue, Donald Trump has said what we've been told is the unsayable—and yet his positions are widely supported by the American people. I well remember when we were told that Ronald Reagan could not defeat Jimmy Carter in 1980, that Reagan was too extreme, that the American people would never elect an actor as president against an experienced politician like Carter. In fact, of course, Ronald Reagan won the 1980 election by sweeping forty-four states, and followed that up with a forty-nine-state landslide reelection in 1984. Reagan was in many ways controversial, unorthodox, and even brash; and he broke the mold for what was considered acceptable in national politics, which turned out to be exactly what voters frustrated by the Carter malaise wanted. Donald Trump is obviously not Ronald Reagan—no one else is—but I do sincerely believe that Donald Trump can remake our politics as Reagan did, give the Republican Party what has eluded them in five of the last six presidential elections—an electoral college *and* popular vote majority—and provide dramatic, conservative reform. I'll show how in the chapters that follow.

CHAPTER 1

Immigration Invasion

The first thing we need to do is secure our southern border—and we need to do it now. We have to stop the flood, and the best way to do that is to build a wall.

—Donald J. Trump

t is important to be clear from the start: The prime motivation behind the Left's support for open borders is not to welcome the oppressed or throw open the doors of opportunity to the huddled masses yearning for a better life. It is a systematic effort to reshape the demographics of the American electorate for benefit of the Democratic Party. The model is California, which, largely through immigration, has been transformed from the "Reagan Country" I well remember to the majority minority far left state it is today, where for the first time in California history, there will not even be a Republican candidate for an open United States Senate seat in November 2016. The choice will be between two liberal Democrats.

The effort to transform America started with Ted Kennedy whose 1965 Immigration Act shifted immigration away from European countries in favor of immigrants from Latin America, Africa, Asia, and the Middle East. In doing so, he helped move immigration away from countries that shared—actually created—America's Western values. Taking their place were immigrants who would help make a more "multicultural" America that liberals could play to their advantage.

"Liberals not only engineered this policy shift but became the chief architects of a taboo against any critical scrutiny of immigration trends and policy, always ready to apply a 'racist' label to dissenters," wrote Otis Graham Jr. in *The Christian Science Monitor*.[1]

Immigration that is in America's national interest is one thing. Immigration that floods our welfare rolls and prisons, and that tears apart our nation's heritage and social fabric is something else.

In the past, immigrants came to America and were grateful for the opportunities they found here, and they accepted American history as a great, inspiring story of patriots and heroes. Now, thanks to the Left, they often view American history as a racist story of "white privilege" and oppression that only big government can undo, where they are entitled to "free" government programs, and in which lawlessness can be justified against allegedly "racist" Republicans. The rioters at Trump rallies who burn American flags, wave foreign ones, and beat up Trump supporters is a vision of what America could become, all with the blessing of the Democratic Party that sees immigration, and the political correctness that prohibits us from talking honestly about immigration, as a way to transform America in the leftist direction that it wants. For decades, the American people have wanted our government to address the crisis of illegal immigration; and yet our government hasn't, except to make matters worse by not enforcing our existing immigration laws, winking at "sanctuary" cities, expanding illegal immigrants' access to social services, and floating proposals for "amnesty" that would grant illegal immigrants citizenship. A poll in the autumn of 2015 found that 61 percent of Americans believe "continued immigration into the country jeopardizes the United States."[2] This is the majority that until now, until Donald Trump, has been left largely voiceless in our halls of government.

"A country that doesn't control its borders can't survive," Trump says. "We are the only country in the world whose immigration system puts the needs of other nations ahead of our own."[3] That must change. Trump has a detailed action plan to address the immigration crisis which is undergirded by these three core principles:[4]

- **A nation without borders is not a nation.** There must be a wall across the southern border.
- **A nation without laws is not a nation.** Laws passed in accordance with our Constitutional system of government must be enforced.
- **A nation that does not serve its own citizens is not a nation.** Any immigration plan must improve jobs, wages, and security for all Americans.

TRUMP'S PLAN

Trump's immigration plan hits the problem from all angles. His comprehensive approach includes the following initiatives:

- **Build a wall along our southern border and make Mexico pay for it.** He proposes that the cost can be covered by increasing existing border fees, raising the price for temporary visas, impounding remittance payments from illegal immigrants, cutting our foreign aid to Mexico, levying tariffs on Mexican products coming into our country, or by convincing the Mexican government that their paying for the wall is a condition of continuing to maintain good relations with the United States.

- **Triple the number of Immigration and Customs Enforcement officers working on the border.** There are only five thousand ICE officers protecting our nation's borders—and they are spread across all fifty states, and the territories of Guam and Puerto Rico. That is half the size of the police force in Los Angeles, but ICE is expected to handle 11 million illegals.
- **Pass nationwide e-verify.** This system guarantees that American employers hire only American citizens or legal immigrants.
- **Mandatory return of all criminal aliens.** The Obama Administration has released 76,000 aliens with criminal convictions since 2013 alone. That's

typical of an administration that seems to care little about protecting the American people. That would change under President Donald Trump, with the American government withholding visas from countries that won't take back their own criminals.

- **Detention—not catch-and-release.** Under Trump's plan, illegal aliens apprehended crossing the border would be detained until they could be sent home, no more nonsensical catch-and-release.

- **Defund sanctuary cities.** Trump would cut-off federal grants to any city that refuses to cooperate with federal law enforcement.

- **End birthright citizenship for anchor babies.**

- **Enhanced penalties for overstaying a visa.** Trump would address the problem of the *millions* of people who come to the United States on temporary visas, and stay. Trump would strengthen the criminal penalties for visa violators and complete the visa tracking system that

is required by law but that has been
blocked by lobbyists.

Trump has been particularly forceful with his
plainspoken affirmation that illegal immigration is
illegal and that, "America will only be great as long
as America remains a nation of laws according to the
Constitution. No one is above the law"—though liberal Democrats routinely act as if illegal immigrants
are above the law and deserving of nearly every right
held by a legal American citizen or resident.

Donald Trump launched his campaign in June
2015 by recognizing that Mexico had sent some of its
worst criminals, murderers, and rapists[5] to live here
illegally. Another truth that few politicians have dared
utter is that illegal immigrants perpetrate a hugely
disproportionate number of serious crimes, with the
estimated 3.5 percent of the population that is here
illegally responsible for 36.7 percent of federal sentences in 2014. As Caroline May reported at Breitbart.
com: "Broken down by some of the primary offenses,
illegal immigrants represented 16.8 percent of drug
trafficking cases, 20.0 percent of kidnapping/hostage
taking, 74.1 percent of drug possession, 12.3 percent
of money laundering, and 12.0 percent of murder
convictions."[6]

But for most Americans, unaware of these statistics, a series of tragic stories in the news highlighted how Trump was right, including most especially the July 1, 2015, murder of Kate Steinle in the sanctuary city of San Francisco by a seven-time convicted felon illegal alien;[7] the July 24, 2015, rape and murder of Marilyn Pharis[8] in her home in Santa Maria, California, by an illegal immigrant who had been arrested no less than six times in the previous fifteen months; and the July 29, 2015, murders of Jason and Tana Shane in Montana and the near-deadly shooting of their daughter by an immigrant who had been allowed into the country under our current lax immigration standards.[9]

Trump has shown the courage of his convictions. Though attacked by the liberal media and by the Left for his criticism of our broken immigration system, he has not backed down. "The countries south of us are not sending us their best people," he has reiterated. "The bad people are coming from places other than just Mexico. They're coming from all over Central and South America, and they're coming probably from the Middle East…This flow of illegal immigrants into this country is one of the most serious problems we face. It's killing us."[10] Trump's bold stance on immigration has given voters the hope that something might finally be done, in a constructive way, about one of the most pressing issues facing this country.

SANCTUARY CITIES

Donald Trump's campaign has shined a national spotlight on the growing problem of "sanctuary cities" that shelter illegal aliens from deportation. According to the Center for Immigration Studies, there are more than 350 jurisdictions in the United States that flout the law by prohibiting the arrest of illegals within their borders.[11] The tragedy of Kate Steinle, who died in the arms of her father after being shot by an illegal alien, in a tourist area of San Francisco, is that her death was preventable, yet officials have defiantly defended their irresponsible sanctuary policies.

It wasn't only the city and county of San Francisco that released the seven-times-convicted, five-times-deported Mexican who killed Kate Steinle; Obama's Immigration and Customs Enforcement let him go, too. ICE has released many thousands of criminal aliens onto unsuspecting local communities instead of returning them to their countries of origin, including 121 who were subsequently charged with murdering Americans between 2011 and 2015. According to government figures compiled by Jessica Vaughan, more than 8,100 deportable aliens (including three thousand felons) were released by sanctuary cities and counties in just the first eight months of 2014, and that number keeps growing since President Obama has ordered federal officials to lay off illegals.[12] Some 1,900 of those wrongly released aliens have already re-offended 4,300 more times, racking up 7,800 new charges including murder, violent assault, rape, and child rape.

The first local sanctuary policy was officially adopted more than thirty years ago. Since then, hundreds of cities and counties have adopted one or more sanctuary policies, such as: refusing to inquire about immigration status when making a traffic stop or other routine police work; refusing to report a subject's unlawful status to the appropriate federal agency (now called ICE); or refusing to honor a "detainer," which is a written request to detain a subject until ICE can deport him. Bills to stop local sanctuary policies were introduced in Congress and state legislatures, but they all wilted under pressure from amnesty advocates, such as businesses dependent on cheap foreign labor.[13] The U.S. House of Representatives finally approved a bill last year to withhold certain federal reimbursements from sanctuary municipalities, but the promise of a presidential veto assures that even this minor reform will never become law.

Headlines proclaim that Republicans voted to "crack down" on sanctuary cities, but nothing will change unless the restrictions are folded into a must-pass appropriations bill.[14] Washington, D.C., for example, remains a sanctuary city even though Congress has the constitutional power "to exercise exclusive legislation in all cases whatsoever" over our nation's capital. Local sanctuary policies protect thousands from deportation, but the real damage is done at the federal level. Policies instituted by the administration of Barack Obama have effectively given sanctuary to millions, thanks to Obama's wholesale refusal to enforce our nation's immigration laws. Take Obama's November 2014 executive amnesty, which would have given legal status and work permits (including Social Security numbers) to approximately 5 million of the estimated 11 million illegal aliens. A brave federal judge blocked the work permits, but the 5 million still benefit from Obama's decision to give them a low enforcement priority, another form of sanctuary. Obama recently extended lower-priority enforcement to several million more people, and approximately 87 percent of the illegal population—all but 1.4 million of the 11 million—are basically home free, as if the United States is now the sanctuary for the whole world.

Don't assume that illegal immigration has stopped just because the official estimate of illegal population has remained steady at 11 to 12 million for a decade. Illegal immigration (which includes people who enter legally but don't go home when their visas expire) continues unabated at the rate of one thousand people per day. During the first six and a half years of the Obama administration, the country took in another 2.5 million illegals. The official numbers have stayed stable by factoring in estimates of "self-deportation" where former illegals have returned across the border. *Legal* immigration is itself a giant factor in America's demographic change. America accepts more than 1.1 million legal immigrants every year. The Census Bureau estimates that "net migration" will bring 14 million new immigrants to the United States during the next ten years. Shouldn't we have some say over our demographic future, of what America is and will become? Shouldn't we have an immigration policy that serves America's national interests? In Europe we have seen the danger of large unassimilated Islamic communities making historic changes in countries and their future; yet we seem blind to similar changes happening here.

Of all Obama's sanctuary policies, probably the worst is his vast expansion of refugee and asylum policies. Largely unnoticed by national media, tens of thousands of so-called refugees, mostly from Muslim countries, are being resettled all over the United States. The United States now receives more refugees than all other countries combined and plops them down in what are called "seed communities" where local opposition is not tolerated. There's even a special federal program to combat "pockets of resistance" such as an uproar in Twin Falls, Idaho, where the U.S. government wants to send three hundred refugees from war-torn Syria.

It is absurd for the United States to continue to bring to our shores populations that bring terrorism with them. We have entire communities now, like the Somalis settled in Minnesota that are recruiting targets for terrorist groups like ISIS. It's time for citizens to stand up and say enough is enough. Islamist terrorism is not native to the United States, but it is here now in incidents ranging from the July 16, 2015, murders of four U.S. Marines and a U.S. Navy sailor in Chattanooga by a Kuwaiti-born Palestinian, to the Boston Marathon bombing by the Tsarnaev brothers in 2013, to the terrorist attack in San Bernadino, California, in December 2015 that killed fourteen people and injured seventeen others. In the aftermath of the Orlando murders, Americans discovered that the radicalized killer was brought up by an immigrant who spewed virulently anti-American talking points of radical Muslims.

Our immigration policies need a major overhaul. Most especially we need immigration policies that protect the safety and security of the people of the United States. If the United States is to remain a nation of laws, cities, counties, and states cannot be allowed to give sanctuary to law breakers. Trump will put a stop to this.

ANCHOR BABIES ON WELFARE

The Pew Research Center has estimated that 340,000 children are born annually to citizens of Mexico and other foreign countries who are living illegally in the United States, and that doesn't include children born to "birth tourists," primarily from Asian countries, which the Center for Immigration Studies estimates could be as high as 36,000.[15] These children are called "anchor babies" because their presumed citizenship enables their parents to access a variety of benefit programs intended for U.S. citizens, and makes it much easier for the entire family to continue living here illegally.

Of all the steps that need to be taken to roll back illegal immigration, "Most important is ending or curtailing so-called birthright citizenship, or anchor babies," Donald Trump says. "That the Fourteenth Amendment has been interpreted to mean that any child born in the United States is automatically an American citizen—and that baby can be used as an anchor to keep its family here—is the single biggest magnet attracting illegal immigrants."[16]

A federal case in Texas could provide a means to stop the practice of extending automatic U.S. citizenship to children born to illegal aliens. The Texas case includes a sworn affidavit from Mexico's consul general for Texas that openly admits that Mexico's official policy is to encourage its poor people to migrate here illegally in order to gain access to our generous welfare system.[17]

Mexico's legal brief, filed in the Texas case, begins by declaring that, "Mexico is responsible to protect its nationals wherever they may be residing," and a footnote clarifies that under the Mexican Constitution, "Mexican nationality is granted to children born abroad of a Mexican born parent." In other words, anchor babies born in this country retain their parents' nationality, which means their citizenship belongs there, not here.

Liberals claim that our own Constitution guarantees automatic U.S. citizenship to all children born on American soil, and it's true that the Fourteenth Amendment begins with the words, "All persons born or naturalized in the United States...are citizens of the United States." But behind those three little dots is an important qualification: "and subject to the jurisdiction thereof." What that forgotten phrase means is that when someone born here is "subject to the jurisdiction" of another nation, that child does not become a U.S. citizen unless the laws passed by Congress so provide (and they don't). By filing its legal brief and submitting sworn testimony in the Texas case, Mexico is officially declaring that children born to its citizens living illegally in the United States remain "subject to the jurisdiction" of Mexico.

The Mexican consul, in his sworn testimony, says that, "My responsibilities in this position include protecting the rights and promoting the interests of my fellow Mexican nationals." He also says, "The main responsibility of consulates is to provide services, assistance, and protection to nationals abroad." Mexico's assertion of continuing jurisdiction over its "nationals abroad" would seem to imply that babies born to Mexican parents in the United States remain, in the eyes of Mexico, Mexican nationals.

The Texas case was filed on behalf of about two dozen Mexican mothers living illegally in Texas. The women complain that without proper ID they cannot get birth certificates for their Texas-born children, and that without birth certificates they can't enroll in Medicaid, food stamps, Section 8 housing, and other U.S. taxpayer-provided benefits.

Like other states, Texas issues a birth certificate to a close relative only upon presentation of a valid ID issued by a U.S. federal or state agency. These restrictions were adopted to combat the growing epidemic of identity theft, often linked to the widespread use of forged or fake documents by illegal aliens. Mexican consulates issue their own official-looking identity document called the *matricula consular*, but Texas refuses to accept it. The basic allegation of the lawsuit is that by refusing to accept the *matricula consular* as proper ID for obtaining a birth certificate, Texas is somehow violating the Fourteenth Amendment.

The Texas lawsuit was concocted by a group called the South Texas Civil Rights Project, which was founded in 1972 as a spin-off of the ACLU. It was assisted by another left-wing legal outfit, Texas Rio Grande Legal Aid, whose largest supporter, the Legal Services Corporation, collected $375 million of U.S. taxpayer funds in 2015. Public opinion is not on the side of the liberal lawyers or their clients, and the courts may be turning against them now too. In October 2015, a federal judge ruled that Texas could deny U.S. birth certificates to the offspring of illegal aliens who don't have *verifiable* (U.S.-issued) identification. This is a start, but leaving the issue to the courts is a risky proposition; better would be what Donald Trump proposes: federal legislation to clarify and affirm that citizenship is not granted automatically to anyone born on U.S. soil.

ENDING "BIRTH TOURISM"

At least 10 percent of all births in the United States every year are babies born to illegal aliens. In fact, there is an entire industry called "birth tourism," offering "birth packages" costing thousands of dollars, that offer to bring pregnant women from all over the world to the United States so that their children can receive "free" medical care, other government benefits, and citizenship (and it's not just Mexicans who are involved; twelve thousand babies from mothers who are Turkish nationals have been born in the United States, by arrangement, since 2003). The brazenness of the business is shocking. An electronic billboard in Mexico, advertising the services of an American doctor, proclaims, "Do you want to have your baby in the U.S.?" The advantages of birthright citizenship are immense. The babies get Medicaid (including birth costs), Temporary Assistance to Needy Families, and food stamps. Obviously, the baby shares his goodies with his family. As soon as the child becomes an adult, he can legalize his parents, and bring into the United States a foreign-born spouse and any foreign-born siblings. They all can then bring in their own extended families, a policy called "chain migration."

Republican Congressman Steve King of Iowa has stepped up to this challenge and already has twenty-seven co-sponsors for his bill, H.R. 140, to define citizenship. It states that the "subject to the jurisdiction" phrase in the Fourteenth Amendment means a baby born in the United States only if at least one parent is a U.S. citizen, or a lawfully-admitted resident alien, or an alien on active duty in the U.S. armed services. Congressman King is not trying to amend the Constitution. He is simply using the Fourteenth Amendment's Section 5, which gives Congress (not the judiciary, not the executive branch), the power to enforce the citizenship clause. In 1993, Nevada Democrat Senator Harry Reid, now the Senate Minority Leader, introduced similar legislation. Bills to limit birthright citizenship to children of U.S. citizens and of aliens who are legal residents have been introduced by other members of Congress every year since. If Donald Trump is elected president, such bills will have executive level support.

With Donald Trump as president, the clear intent of the Fourteenth Amendment can be reinforced. The Fourteenth Amendment, ratified in 1868, was designed to overturn the *Dred Scott* decision in which the U.S. Supreme Court declared that African-Americans could not be citizens. It had nothing to do with offering citizenship to the children of foreign nationals. In fact, the Fourteenth Amendment did not even apply to American Indians, because they were "subject to the jurisdiction" of their tribal governments. Congress did not grant citizenship to American Indians on reservations until 1924, fifty-six years later.

The United States does not recognize dual citizenship—such as the Mexican consulate in Texas claims for the children of Mexican nationals born in the United States. To become a U.S. citizen, immigrants are required to swear allegiance and renounce any allegiance to the nation from which they came.

The solemn oath that all naturalized Americans must take has no ambiguity: "I hereby declare, on oath, that I absolutely and entirely renounce and abjure all allegiance and fidelity to any foreign prince, potentate, state, or sovereignty, of whom or which I have heretofore been a subject or citizen so help me God." More than a hundred years ago, Theodore Roosevelt campaigned against the idea of "hyphenated" Americans. Donald Trump is raising that banner again.

AMERICAN JOBS FOR AMERICAN WORKERS

Donald Trump is a nationalist. He wants American jobs to be held by American workers. Only about half of our science, technology, engineering, and math (STEM) college graduates find high-tech jobs in

STEM-related fields. Why? Because businesses use H-1B visas to hire lower cost foreign nationals to do these jobs. These immigrants aren't doing jobs that Americans won't do, they are quite literally taking jobs from Americans, as recently happened when 250 skilled technical employees of the Walt Disney Company in Florida were laid off after being forced to train their foreign replacements recruited under the H-1B program.

Donald Trump has pledged to stop this abuse of the H-1B program, and to crack down on foreign workers who stay in the United States under expired visas. And he has faced up to the reality, which few Republicans or Democrats want to do, that if the United States wants to clean up its immigration mess it will have to enforce the law with deportations. As is so often the case with necessary reform, we're told this is impossible, even though we did it successfully in the past. President Dwight Eisenhower peacefully removed at least 1 million illegal aliens in June 1954 and sent them back to Mexico. Many got the message and left on their own. We have to do that again, and Trump will push Congress to get it done.

The issues of immigration and jobs are naturally intertwined. The wages of working Americans have been stagnant for many years, and part of the reason is our high levels of immigration (both legal and illegal) and the many different guest worker programs. It's about time we had a president who put American workers first. Donald Trump will do that.

FIGHTING BORDER CRIME

Border crime is a huge problem, and Trump's plan to regain control of our borders would put an equally huge dent in it. As William C. Triplet II, a former chief Republican counsel to the Senate Foreign Relations Committee, has pointed out, if Trump wins, the drug cartels lose. He notes that "The two groups with the most to lose with a Donald Trump victory on November 8 would be the Mexican drug cartels and their Chinese suppliers. The reason is pretty simple: Mr. Trump has made securing the border his principal campaign theme. If the border is secured by a wall or some combination of means against the flood of illegal aliens and potential terrorists, then it automatically puts a major hit on the flow of narcotics across the border. If they can't get the illegals in, they can't get the dope in, either." That would be a great development for both the United States *and* Mexico.[18]

GETTING SERIOUS

The United States we remember was a melting pot. Immigrants, almost entirely from Europe, came here to become Americans, to assimilate into the American nation-state and our American way of life. An American was a definable person, recognizable to all. To be an American was to be a hard-working, law-abiding, church or synagogue-attending, person who probably thought of himself as middle class or aspiring to middle class respectability. The old movies and TV shows are nostalgic but they reveal a great truth of who we are as Americans. And, even though Americans welcomed many to the melting pot, we also took long pauses to allow the assimilation to take place. Those long periods where relatively few immigrants came at all were part of the American plan.

The number of immigrants living in this country has jumped from less than 10 million in 1970 to more than 42 million in 2014, and that is not counting the millions of illegal immigrants within our borders. It would be a challenge for any society to absorb and assimilate that many immigrants, coming from all corners of the world, but the task is made even harder when the Left *discourages* assimilation in favor of multiculturalism. "Uncontrolled immigration threatens to deconstruct the nation we grew up in and convert America into a conglomeration of peoples with almost nothing in common—no history, heroes, language, culture, faith, or ancestors," warned Pat

Buchanan in his bestselling book, *The Death of the West*, "Balkanization beckons."[19]

"How can we feel good about handing over this mess to our children and grandchildren? How can we think about the hundreds of thousands of soldiers, sailors, airmen, and Marines who have died for our freedom and way of life and not be ashamed at how we've let their gift to be trashed and abused?" asks Donald Trump. "If we're going to turn this thing around, we have to do it fast."[20] He's right. The revolution starts here, and it starts with returning sanity to U.S. immigration policy that returns America to Americans.

CHAPTER 2

Rotten Trade Deals

*Open markets are the ideal, but if one guy is cheating the
whole time, how is that free trade?*

—Donald J. Trump

"I want to be clear, this is strictly a business decision," the suit said coldly to hundreds of workers huddled around the factory floor on February 9, 2016.[1] The bad news was that Carrier Corporation was closing its two manufacturing plants in Indiana, laying off 2,100 workers, and sending their middle-class jobs building air-conditioning units to Mexico. "The fact is, what will drive world-class margins, why margins at our climate-control and security business are so good, is because we have been relentless in taking out costs," Greg Hayes, CEO of Carrier's parent company United Technologies, told investors. A more accurate term for the "costs" that are relentlessly being cut would be "U.S. jobs." Donald Trump reacted to the layoffs from the campaign trail. "I'm going to tell the head of Carrier: 'I hope you enjoy your stay in Mexico, folks. But every single unit that you make and send across our border, you're going to pay a 35 percent tax.'" Trump says U.S. businesses need to prioritize keeping jobs in America after decades of fleeing overseas.

"I'm sick of always reading about outsourcing," Trump wrote in his 2011 book, *Time to Get Tough*. "Why aren't we talking about 'onshoring'? We need to bring manufacturing jobs back home where they belong. Onshoring, or 'repatriation,' is a way for us to take back the jobs China is stealing."[2] No matter what it's called or where they end up, millions of jobs have been shipped overseas by U.S. companies looking for dirt cheap labor. Studies suggest that immediate cost savings can be as high as 40 percent when companies lay off American workers and move their jobs abroad.[3] The consequence is 6 million offshored jobs since 2001, with more than 3 million of those positions being shipped to Communist China. Contrary to common views, the layoffs don't only affect blue-collar industrial jobs but positions across all sectors of the economy. "Almost every employer seems to be doing it," reports *Crain's Chicago Business* about recent

offshoring by Illinois companies. "Engineers in Scha-
umburg, cookie bakers in Chicago, and medical-
device makers in Downers Grove are among those
who have been laid off because their work was
exported."[4] This is a trend that has hollowed out
towns across America's industrial heartland, especially in the Midwest.

Bad trade deals that sell out American workers
just keep coming. The latest trade scheme is the
Trans-Pacific Partnership, commonly known as the
TPP. The granddaddy of all trade deals, it involves a
dozen nations combining to form one unified trade
zone similar to what exists in the European Union.
There is one major difference, however, in that the
TPP throws together a handful of First World nations
with high wages into the mix with Third World
developing economies with extremely low pay scales.
On the high end of the TPP, there is the United States,
Japan, Canada, Australia, Singapore, and New Zea-
land; on the low end is Mexico, Vietnam, Malaysia,
Peru, Chile, and Brunei. Consider that the average
annual income in the United States is over $52,000[5]
compared to only $1,890 in Vietnam.[6] It doesn't take
much imagination to guess in which direction the
jobs will be outsourced in this relationship. In the
1992 election, Ross Perot won 20 percent of the vote
as a third-party candidate for president by warning

about "the giant sucking sound" that would be heard as jobs were flushed out of America due to the North American Free Trade Agreement (NAFTA). That controversial trade deal, which eradicated trade barriers between Mexico, the United States, and Canada, only included 25 percent of the markets of the much larger TPP, which is the most ambitious trade zone ever concocted.

The five years of negotiations to hammer out this six-thousand-page TPP deal were conducted under the strictest secrecy, and thanks to the Republican Congress inexplicably giving President Obama Fast Track trade-negotiating authority in June 2015, there will be no congressional oversight of the deal.[7] The Senate, with a GOP majority, passed the Fast Track measure by a 60 to 38 vote to surrender its input in trade deals. Fast Track consolidates power in the executive branch and eliminates Congress' constitutional power to amend or even debate trade legislation.[8] Fast Track allows only a specified up-or-down vote on momentous international agreements such as the TPP.

Like the TPP, by its very essence, Fast Track turns over some of our authority as a sovereign nation to international authorities, which is a major longtime goal of internationalists and business lobbyists who dream about there being one global community with no borders, where products and people can move

jobs in America.[11] Those negative numbers will increase exponentially in future years as the agreement settles in. When you break down the numbers, even using the TPP's proponents' bogus numbers, the supposed benefits still are not lavish at all. The ostensible spike in GDP only amounts to one extra month of economic growth over fifteen years than would occur without the TPP, the new jobs that are counted can be part-time jobs, and even these would not be enough to qualify for what is considered to be a positive increase in employment on a month-to-month basis under normal conditions. In other words, not even a federal propaganda machine can spin this deal to predict real benefits for the U.S. economy or U.S. workers. In fact, the ITC report is upfront about predicting that the TPP will lead to even more lost U.S. manufacturing jobs. The sectors that will be hit hardest are far-ranging and include layoffs in such diverse industries that sell electronic equipment, auto parts, medical devices, industrial machinery, leather goods, wood products, textiles, and chemicals.[12]

Negative fallout from previous trade deals presages similar trouble ahead with the TPP. Take the 2012 free-trade deal with South Korea known as KORUS that was passed by huge majorities from both parties in Congress and signed by President Obama. By 2015, the U.S. trade deficit with South Korea jumped by 115

percent, or more than $15 billion.[13] In just four short
years, our trade deficit with South Korea more than
doubled. Contrary to the pretense that so-called free
trade is a two-way street, during the first four years
after this agreement was signed, imports from South
Korea to the United States grew by 27 percent while
there was zero reciprocal growth in American products being sold in South Korea. In the first month
alone after the deal went into effect, U.S. exports to
South Korea fell by 12 percent as our trade deficit
tripled.[14] This raw deal has cost at least one hundred
thousand U.S. jobs. Obama had said that at least seventy thousand new U.S. jobs would result from $10
to $11 billion in new U.S. exports to Korea. Instead,
as Donald Trump has lamented, "We're giving away
the greatest market in the world—the American consumer."[15]

Detroit, the former "Arsenal of Democracy" that
churned out the tanks, planes, jeeps, and other
machinery that won World War II, has been hit particularly hard by bad trade deals. Now that Korean
automobile manufacturers have freer access to our
market, a whopping 85 percent of the increase in the
U.S. trade deficit with Korea has been in lost sales of
U.S. cars and auto parts.[16] Many Korean cars are
deceptively marketed as "Made in the U.S.A." because
final assembly occurs in a U.S. facility, but a majority

of parts that go into every one of these vehicles are produced in and shipped here from Korea, not made by U.S. domestic suppliers.[17] The recent rise of the Korean auto industry, which has grown by $10.6 billion in import sales to America in the four years leading up to 2015, has been at the expense of domestic manufacturers that U.S. trade negotiators, Congress, and President Obama gave short shrift. The devastation to our auto industry will escalate in five years when all remaining protections on U.S. cars will be repealed as a final condition of KORUS being fully implemented.

If the far-reaching TPP is the granddaddy of all rotten trade deals, NAFTA is the deadbeat dad who always makes promises but never delivers on them. The North American Free Trade Agreement lifted trade barriers between Mexico, the United States, and Canada. Between 1994, when NAFTA went into force, and the end of 2014, the U.S. trade deficit with our free-trade partners leapt by 430 percent. "Since Fast Track trade authority was used to pass NAFTA and the U.S. entrance into the World Trade Organization, the overall annual U.S. trade deficit in goods has more than quadrupled, from $218 billion to $912 billion," reports Reuters. NAFTA is estimated to have robbed U.S. small businesses of more than $27 billion in exports to the bordering Canadian and Mexican markets; and of course hardest hit has been the American working class. "Three of every five displaced manufacturing workers rehired in 2014 are earning lower wages, according to the Bureau of Labor Statistics, with one-third taking a pay cut greater than 20 percent," explains Leo Hindery Jr., the former CEO of AT&T Broadband. "U.S. workers without college degrees have lost roughly 12.2 percent of their wages—even after accounting for the benefits of cheaper imported goods. This means *less,* not more, consumer demand for U.S. man-ufacturing and service-sector firms."[18] Nevertheless, U.S. politicians persist in pushing for more, and much larger, trade deals.

Before Donald Trump, there had been no effective national political spokesman for the American worker. Now there is. Trump states unequivocally that, "Trade deals are absolutely killing our country." An increas-ingly large majority of Americans agree with him. According to a June 2015 *New York Times/CBS News* poll, 63 percent agreed with the statement that, "trade restrictions are necessary to protect domestic industries," and only 30 percent felt that, "free trade must be allowed even if domestic industries are hurt by foreign competition."[19] A growing number of Americans no longer feel the economic system works for them and are expressing frustration that they are being locked out of the global economy by our own corporations and our own politicians. The outpouring of support in this election for Donald Trump, and to a certain degree for Bernie Sanders in the Democratic primaries as well, is a manifestation of this frustration and the feeling that establishment politicians do not care or are not even aware of the plight of regular people across the country.

Generations of Americans have believed that if they worked hard they could improve their economic standing and give a better future to their children. By blithely trading away American jobs, especially blue collar jobs, in order to pursue free trade and its alleged benefits for the consumer, our political class has left many Americans no longer believing that the American Dream is within their grasp; instead, they find themselves shunted out of well-paying manufacturing jobs and into lower paid service jobs. Consider the following:[20]

- In 2010, median family income was 6 percent lower than it was in 2000. In this ten-year period, family income dropped to $62,301 from $66,259 while the cost of living increased during that time.
- Between 2000 and 2010, the hourly wage of workers with college and

high-school diplomas remained stagnant, even as their productivity increased by 22 percent.

- Since 1973, median hourly compensation has risen by 11 percent, while the productivity of the American worker has increased by 80 percent.
- Those with wages in the lowest 10th percentile saw their 2011 income drop below the level of 1979.
- Meanwhile, life is good for corporate bosses who are offshoring millions of jobs and suppressing salaries for whatever positions that remain here. Forty years ago, average CEO pay was thirty times that of the typical employee; in the last five years it has skyrocketed to two hundred times the employee average.

A lot of conservatives will argue that this is just how markets work. As one law review article puts it: "In order for new industries to be born, old industries must be allowed to die."[21] As the economy changes, some sectors grow, new ones are created, and other industries die off or move somewhere else, but in international trade, there is no such thing as a truly free market; political decisions inevitably favor some industries over others, and some companies over others—in many cases the beneficiaries are foreign firms, workers, and governments. But the ideologues tend to ignore that, or downplay it, or say that countries that play such political games only hurt themselves in the long run, though that remains to be seen. Here's the theory: "Trade liberalization is about expanding markets across national boundaries and broadening the scope for specialization and economies of scale—the essential ingredients of wealth creation," a recent policy paper published by the libertarian Cato Institute says. "When trade barriers come down, the factory floor can span borders and oceans, which enables production to be organized in new and more efficient formats."[22] In fact, factory floors don't "span borders and oceans." That's a fancy and disingenuous way of saying the factory jobs get sent to China or Mexico.

The conservative position should be to defend America—its jobs, its prosperity, and its national security. Phony free trade doesn't do that. It is easy to gloss over free trade's costs by saying that consumers benefit (though that is not always the case) or that American workers just need to become more productive (as we've seen they are, but have not benefited) or produce goods that other countries want to buy, but the fact is that the United States and the American worker are getting the short end of our current free trade deals.

As financial theorist William J. Bernstein notes, "The pain and dislocation in the lives of individuals, industries, and nations caused by the globalization of the planet's economy are real." The interests of the rest of the world are not always in sync with America's interests, and when that's the case, American leaders need to put America first. "America will stage a comeback, and our next comeback must be led by people who know what works and what doesn't," Donald Trump says.[23] "What we need is a strong leader who knows how to negotiate, and who understands how business works and how businesses are built."[24]

THE CHINA THREATS

Donald Trump has made a point of challenging Communist China on its three main threats to the United States: currency manipulation, a systematic effort to destroy our manufacturing base, and industrial espionage and cyber warfare. As president, Donald Trump promises to:[25]

1. **Bring China to the bargaining table** by immediately declaring it a currency manipulator.

2. **Protect American ingenuity and investment** by forcing China to uphold intellectual property laws and stop their unfair and unlawful practice of forcing U.S. companies to share proprietary technology with Chinese competitors as a condition of entry to China's market.

3. **Reclaim millions of American jobs and revive American manufacturing** by putting an end to China's illegal export subsidies and lax labor and environmental standards. No more sweatshops or pollution havens stealing jobs from American workers.

4. **Strengthen our negotiating position** by lowering our corporate tax rate to keep American companies and jobs here at home, attacking our debt and deficit so China cannot use financial blackmail against us, and bolstering the U.S. military presence in the East and South China Seas to discourage Chinese adventurism.

In his important book *The Great Betrayal*, Pat Buchanan argues that, "Free trade is shredding the society we grew up in and selling out America's sovereignty...free trade is truly a betrayal of Middle America and treason to the vision of the Founding Fathers."[26] And not to mention the Republican Party, which began its life, under Abraham Lincoln, as the party of protection, tariffs, and putting American jobs and businesses first.

Today, standing up for American jobs and American industry is yet another way for Donald Trump to strip support away from Hillary Clinton, who is on the record as a supporter of globalist free trade. In 2012, Hillary crowed that the TPP "sets the gold standard in trade agreements" and praised TPP at least forty-five times in speeches and other prepared remarks.[27] Under pressure from Bernie Sanders, she's been fudging her position, but Trump speaks for America on this issue. Hillary doesn't.

A May 2015 Ipsos Public Affairs poll found that 84 percent of Americans believe that "protecting American manufacturing jobs is more important than getting Americans access to more products."[28] A June 2015 *NBC News* poll revealed that 66 percent of Americans believe that "protecting American industries and jobs by limiting imports from other countries is more important than allowing free trade so you can buy products at low prices no matter what country they come from." The sentiment is even stronger among unaffiliated voters. According to a 2012 survey by the Mellman Group and North Star Opinion Research, 87 percent of independent voters support "Buy American" policies. Only 17 percent think free-trade agreements create jobs here at home. Between 1999 and 2010, the number of Americans who said that free-trade agreements "hurt the United States" rose more than twenty points to 53 percent from 32 percent.

As these polls illustrate, America is more than a nation of consumers, wanting cheap products; it is a nation of workers; a nation that wants economic security just as much as it wants border security.

"So how do we get back the jobs we've lost to other countries?" Trump asked rhetorically in his book *Crippled America*. "Answer: Start by negotiating better trade agreements with our 'friendly' partners. We have to bring jobs back from places like China, Japan, and Mexico. We have to stand up and be tough."[29] Trump is right that America needs to negotiate better trade deals that will benefit our own workers and industries. Combined with a concerted effort to slash and repeal regulations that penalize American companies and a tax-cutting policy lifted straight from Ronald Reagan's era of robust growth, we believe that Donald Trump will turn America's economy around.

CHAPTER 3

Political Correctness Kills

The big problem this country has is being politically correct.

—Donald J. Trump

I vanka Trump just puts it out there. "My father's not politically correct, he says what he means and he means what he says, and I think that's the way the American people are."[1] She's right. Polls consistently show that upwards of 80 percent of Americans believe that political correctness is a serious problem crippling the nation, though significantly only 35 percent of Democrats do.[2] For liberals, political correctness has become one of the most important ways they advance their agenda—they simply dismiss their opponents as bigots. All too often, Republicans play along with this game and thus let Democrats dictate the terms of debate, which explains why Republican electoral victories don't often lead to conservative policy victories.

But now, at last, the American people have a candidate for president who not only shares their concerns but is determined to do something about them, regardless of what the liberal media, leftist politicians, or establishment Republicans say.

THE TYRANNY OF POLITICAL CORRECTNESS

On college campuses today, freedom of speech and thought are practically endangered species. Left-wing colleges and universities have even set aside "free speech zones"—small, limited areas where conservatives can enjoy a sharply curtailed right to free speech. And what the Left has done to our college campuses it wants to do to America at large. It wants, through social pressure—but also through laws and court edicts—to rule conservative ideas out of bounds, as impermissible thought and speech.

We've seen some of these battles in the realm of fights over religious freedom, and whether small business-owners can publicly follow their Christian conscience. We've seen it through the action of leftist politicians and attorneys general who want to outlaw skepticism of global warming. It has gotten so bad that even some liberals find themselves protesting against it. Liberal commentator Kirsten Powers has condemned the Left's "illiberal intolerance and intimidation" and written an entire book about it called *The Silencing: How the Left Is Killing Free Speech.*

Donald Trump is famously politically incorrect. He is not one to let his voice be stifled. He will not limit his truth-telling to small "free-speech zones." He will not accept politically correct limits on what he can say and think.

Many Republicans think this is an embarrassment. Instead, they should see it for what it really is: a strength.

Yes, certainly Donald Trump sometimes responds to insults in kind, or says something poorly worded or clumsy that we wish he hadn't, but at a bare minimum he cuts through the fog of political correctness that blinds even many conservatives.

Economist and columnist Stephen Moore was exactly right when he noted that all politicians say stupid or offensive things, but Democrats—with the help of the Democrat-friendly media—brush their stupid comments aside and move on, while Republicans actually amplify their mistakes, criticizing their own in extreme terms, pandering to the political correctness of the Left.

Republicans, as Moore rightly says, are too often "pathetic wimps," willing to throw their fellow Republicans, especially Donald Trump, under the bus, so that they can preen before the media and say, "See how racially progressive I am? I just denounced Donald Trump. He's the Republican racist, not me."

As Moore notes,

> When Trump was absurdly charged with not properly denouncing…a white supremacist, even many conservatives responded with leftist attacks. He wasn't sufficiently apologetic for the liberal media, and some Republicans, such as…Mitt Romney, nearly called him a member of the Ku Klux Klan…
>
> All of this is self-defeating on many levels…Since when do we judge our candidates based on the left's warped criteria? These Republicans seem to suffer from Stockholm syndrome, seeking the affection of their captors…. Trump can win millions of votes of economically left-behind minorities in record numbers this year. But that won't happen by genuflecting to the left-wing civil-rights leadership. And it won't happen if the GOP's leadership is calling their flag bearer a racist.[3]

Trump—unlike the establishment Republicans Moore properly condemns—has no interest in playing by the liberal media's rules or taking his talking points from the Left. Like no president since Ronald Reagan, Trump will come into office with his own plan, his own agenda—one that pays no mind to the agenda of the political establishment or the enforcers of political correctness. He is quite happy to say what he thinks whether it is politically correct or not—and he will speak politically incorrect truths that no one else will say.

Donald Trump can help conservatives with truth-telling on a wide variety of issues where the Left is trying to silence us. Here are some examples.

GLOBAL COOLING

A 2015 poll exposed that 27 percent—more than one-quarter—of Democrats support the federal government prosecuting scientists and institutions that question so-called global warming.[4] During the summer of 2016, a group of Democratic congressmen led by Maxine Waters of California declared that First Amendment rights to free speech don't protect global warming skeptics, who they said should be prosecuted.[5]

Silencing the other side of the issue, and thus squelching debate, is the whole point of political correctness. The left-wing attorney general of the Virgin Islands is tripping over himself to rattle off subpoenas targeted at conservative and libertarian think tanks that undertake research that counters the ivory tower's line that global warming is caused primarily by human-generated carbon emissions. Making his agenda clear at a press conference with Al Gore, Claude Walker pledged to Greenpeace activists that he would use his prosecutorial power to do something "transformational" to roll back the use of fossil fuels, which he claims are "destroying the earth."[6] Walker hoped to stifle the right to free speech of such organizations as the Institute for Energy Research, the Competitive Enterprise Institute, the Cato Institute, the Heritage Foundation, and the Heartland Institute. Oil giant ExxonMobil is also being sued for funding research that supports its business interests, which would seem to be an obvious right for a company facing enormously expensive and dubious regulations.

A two-bit ambulance chaser in a tiny place like the Virgin Islands taking on Exxon might seem like the mouse that roared, but the cost of defending a case against government officials can be cripplingly high, especially for groups that don't have the resources of an energy conglomerate. Mounting scientific evidence that the planet is not warming, or warming only mildly, or is even actually cooling is either ignored or outright suppressed. In 2009, a group of climate scientists were busted for apparently fudging data when an email was leaked instructing colleagues to "hide the decline" in global temperatures used to justify their global-warming theories; they sued critics to silence discussion of the scandal.[7] Trump won't be cowed so easily. "This very expensive global-warming [B.S.] has got to stop," he's tweeted. "Our planet is freezing, record low temps, and our GW scientists are stuck in ice."[8]

Donald Trump is definitely not captive to the green lobby or the global warming lobby, and will most definitely not use the power of the federal government to stifle scientific debate and discussion and alternative points of view.

DON'T YOU DARE CRITICIZE MURDEROUS MUSLIMS

Nowhere is the suicidal nature of political correctness more glaring than in the case of Islam. America and the civilized world are under attack from a radicalized global ideology that wants to destroy us. Yet the Obama administration refuses to confront this fact, and will not even utter the words "Islamic extremism." As national security expert Dr. Sebastian Gorka has pointed out in his book *Defeating Jihad,* to defeat our enemies, we have to be able to name them, to know who they are, what motivates them, and what their goals are. Unfortunately, in the case of Islamist terrorism, political correctness—enforced by liberals and the Obama administration—prevents that.

A perfect example came in June 2016 when a Muslim terrorist went on a shooting rampage at a homosexual bar in Orlando, Florida, killing or injuring more than a hundred people. Donald Trump responded to the outrage, and Democratic and liberal media comments about it, by saying:

> The media talks about "homegrown," terrorism, but Islamic radicalism, and the networks that nurture it, are imports from overseas.
>
> Yes, there are many radicalized people already inside our country as a result of the poor policies of the past. But the whole point is that it will be much, much easier to deal with our current problem if we don't keep on bringing in people who add to the problem.
>
> For instance, the controversial Mosque attended by the Boston Bombers had as its founder an immigrant from overseas charged in an assassination plot.

This shooter in Orlando was the child of an immigrant father who supported one of the most repressive regimes on Earth. Why would we admit people who support violent hatred?

Hillary Clinton…continues to support immigration policies that bring Islamic extremists to our country who suppress women, gays and anyone who doesn't share their views.

She can't have it both ways. She can't claim to be supportive of these communities while trying to increase the number of people coming in who want to oppress them.

How does this kind of immigration make our life better? How does this kind of immigration make our country better?

Why does Hillary Clinton want to bring people here—in vast numbers—who reject our values?

I don't want them in our country.[9]

Have you ever heard such plain-speaking from a politician before?

"Why would we admit people who support violent hatred?"

"Why does Hillary Clinton want to bring people here—in vast numbers—who reject our values?"

"How does this kind of immigration make our life better? How does this kind of immigration make our country better?"

These are hugely relevant questions that the American people ask themselves every day—and that politicians rarely, if ever, address.

Many establishment Republicans considered Trump's reaction an embarrassment, almost as much as the Democrats did, because they are equally ideologically wedded to mass immigration and denying that Islam has an inherent problem with radicalism.

The reaction of the Left and the mainstream media and establishment Republicans to the jihadist attack in Orlando was telling. The killer, Omar Mateen, had pledged allegiance to the Islamic State (ISIS), traveled to Saudi Arabia on religious pilgrimage, and screamed "Allahu Akbar" as he gunned down partygoers, laughing while he was killing.[10] The response from the Left was predictable and pathetic. Facebook rushed to shut down the webpage of known Islam critic Pamela Geller,[11] Twitter was accused of censoring the popular hashtag #GaysForTrump, conservative blogger Milo Yiannopoulos's Twitter account was suspended for his comments on Islam,[12] and other social-media gagged their users in similar fashion. In a televised statement the next day, President Obama yapped about the need for gun control, celebrated the LGBTQ (lesbian, gay, bisexual, transgender, questioning) community, said the American public had a lot of "soul-searching" to do, and lectured Americans on how to treat one another but did not utter a single word about Islam, ISIS, the Islamic State or the hateful jihadist mentality that was the source and motivation for the largest terrorist attack in America since September 11, 2001.

Indeed, Obama claimed that the nightclub where the victims were attacked "is more than a nightclub—it is a place of solidarity and empowerment where people have come together to raise awareness, to speak their minds, and advocate for their civil rights."[13] It seems doubtful that many in the nightclub were debating civil rights at two in the morning, and the president's message seemed even more off-base when it was revealed that the killer himself was a member of the "LGBTQ community" and a regular at the nightclub.

Facing facts is not a strong point of the Left, and since they couldn't even say the words "radical Islam"—let alone acknowledge a homosexual Islamist jihadist who was a registered Democrat—they bizarrely, but predictably turned to attacking Donald Trump, essentially blaming his truth-telling on immigration for the attacks, just as they earlier blamed his stance on immigration for rioters who attacked his supporters at Trump rallies in California, with the Democrat mayor of San Jose, California, whose own police had been attacked and who had witnessed Trump supporters being harassed, chased, and beaten, saying, "At some point, Donald Trump needs to take responsibility for the irresponsible behavior of his campaign."[14] Talk about blaming the victim!

The *New York Times* wanted to blame Republicans for the Orlando shooting, because they allegedly see bigotry "as something to exploit, not to extinguish." Other leftist outlets wanted to target "toxic masculinity" or guns[15] or even Christians[16] who hold traditional beliefs on sexual morality. And even Republicans seemed to take a perverse pleasure in insisting the Orlando killer was born in America and therefore Muslim immigration was not a problem—a non sequitur if ever there was one, because as Trump rightly pointed out, it is often the children of immigrants who become terrorists. Everyone who studies this issue knows this, but political correctness apparently prohibits many Republicans from saying it. Somehow it was perfectly acceptable for Democrats to turn the Orlando shooting into an excuse to call for more restrictions on the Second Amendment, just as they turned the Charleston shooting into a hysterical, iconoclastic war against the Confederate battle flag, Confederate statues and monuments, and slave-holding presidents like George Washington, Thomas Jefferson, and Andrew Jackson. But it was somehow wrong, rude, and unpresidential for Donald Trump to question why we are allowing immigration to our country of people from areas of the world that are prone to jihadist violence. Obama has spun multicultural fantasies about how Islam has been a part of American history from the beginning. Trump is right, that jihadist violence is not an "American" problem; it is a problem we have brought to our country through wrong-headed immigration policies. Our inability to confront this reality confirms something else Trump has said: "Political correctness is deadly."

Donald Trump was one of the very few voices, and certainly the most important one, willing to tell it like it was. The president, he said, sounded "more angry at me than the shooter," and added pointedly: "We have a radical Islamic Terrorism problem [even if] we pretend like Obama that we don't."[17]

Conservatives who profess to be unafraid to name our enemy—Islamist terrorism—should be no less unafraid to come to the logical conclusion that Muslim immigration to this country needs to be carefully examined, especially as we know that al-Qaeda and ISIS and other terror groups are looking to exploit

America's and Europe's porous borders. Failing to do so is suicide through political correctness.

AGENTS OF LUCIFER

The rise of Donald Trump and his straight talk has stirred up a hornet's nest of buzzing about a perceived decline in civility in politics. Part of this chatter is based on ignorance of how rough-and-tumble the American political arena has been, such as in the 19th century when guns were brandished in Congress and Representative Preston Brooks almost beat Senator Charles Sumner to death with a cane on the Senate floor over a dispute about a speech. Another part of this narrative is peddled by milquetoast establishmentarians in Congress who prefer to go along to get along and not rock the boat much. They are comfortable in their taxpayer-supported lifestyles and frequently genuflect to a mythical better time in the past when bipartisanship reigned and Democrats and Republicans met each other halfway on legislation. Even if that congressional utopia ever existed (which it didn't), the situation today is markedly different because the survival of the nation is at stake. And one side is determined to ruin America.

It is vital to understand exactly why the 2016 election is so consequential. The explanation goes back to

leafy Wellesley, Massachusetts, where the 2016 Democrat candidate for president, Hillary Clinton, was an
undergraduate student. A young, idealistic hippie,
Hillary wrote her senior honors thesis on Marxist-
anarchist agitator Saul Alinsky, whom she admired
and maintained a private correspondence with until
his death. Her mentor's groundbreaking 1971 primer
on fomenting social disruption, *Rules for Radicals,*
was dedicated to Satan. As impossible as this sounds,
it's true, and it reveals how far out there Hillary is.
Alinsky praises "the first radical known to man who
rebelled against the establishment and did it so effectively that he at least won his own kingdom—LUCI-
FER."[18]

That *Rules for Radicals* honored Lucifer is a
reminder that, as Russell Kirk noted in his classic
book, *The Conservative Mind*, "Political problems,
at bottom, are religious and moral problems."[19]

Or to put it a different way, all politics is a battle
between good and evil.

Perhaps this idea was best expressed by Archbishop
Charles Chaput who said in January 2014, in remarks
addressed to the March for Life: "Evil talks a lot about
'tolerance' when it's weak. When evil is strong, real
tolerance gets pushed out the door. And the reason is
simple. Evil cannot bear the counter-witness of truth.
It will not co-exist peacefully with goodness, because

evil insists on being seen as right, and *worshiped* as being right. Therefore, the good must be made to seem hateful and wrong."[20]

That's a pretty good description of political correctness, which proclaims its own tolerance while being utterly intolerant of every other point of view. This attitude of the Left is not new; William F. Buckley Jr. noted it long ago when he defined a liberal as someone who claimed to be open to all points of view—and then was surprised (and outraged) that there *were* other points of view.

If Hillary Clinton is elected, this liberal intolerance will reach ever higher levels of stridency and persecution. While feeble establishment Republicans talk about bipartisanship and working in good faith with liberal Democrats, the Left aims for total victory, which includes utterly discrediting, if not annihilating, its opponents. Political correctness plays a big part in this; and as it solidifies its control over our schools and our media, let alone our politics, conservatives are going to find themselves ever more embattled.

Alinsky advised his followers: "The major premise for tactics is the development of operations that will maintain a constant pressure upon the opposition. Pick the target, freeze it, personalize it, and polarize it."[21]

The Left does this all the time. Clueless Republicans all too often go along—always ready to try to curry favor with liberals and the mainstream media by capitulating whenever the Left picks its target, freezes it, personalizes it, and polarizes it. Rich Lowry in a short piece for *National Review*'s "The Corner" titled "Behold the Cultural Power of the Left," wrote:

> On the [debate about the] Confederate battle flag [in the wake of the Charleston church shootings], we are once again witnessing the sheer cultural power of the Left: take an irrelevancy (or at the very least a sideshow), make it the central, all-consuming issue, move the debate with astonishing speed, and then, after achieving the initial victory (in this case, removing the flag from the grounds of the South Carolina state capitol), demand yet more (now Walmart and other retailers aren't going to sell Confederate-flag paraphernalia and there will be a broader assault on anything associated with the Confederacy). This is the grinding wheel of the Left's cultural war in action.[22]

So it goes with "the war on women," "the one percent," and the Left's attempt to rule Donald Trump's truth-telling out of bounds.

Of General Ulysses S. Grant, Lincoln said, "I need him, he fights." Of Donald Trump, Americans increasingly believe, "We need him. He says what he means and means what he says. He speaks the truth." Trump is not afraid to speak the truth about radical Islam, or global warming, or anything else. He fearlessly tells the truth as he sees it, and nothing at this point in our history is more important. "We've become so politically correct that we don't know what the hell we're doing," Trump fumes.[23] His frustration is a promising sign that he would take on this enemy of freedom of thought, speech, and religion. Just as Ronald Reagan dispelled the malaise of the Carter years, Trump, we expect, will free America from the political correctness that is destroying our nation's cultural, intellectual, and political life. To remove the gag orders on our most fundamental freedoms, we need a defender of liberty in the White House. Donald Trump is that man, and he deserves the vote of every true conservative.

CHAPTER 4

Restraining Judicial Activism

I'm not appointing a liberal judge.

—Donald J. Trump

The next president of the United States most likely will appoint three or four justices to the U.S. Supreme Court. Love it or hate it (we hate it), judges are the ones setting the agenda for America, and by legislating from the bench, they are the chief architects of national life. This is not how the Founders devised our constitutional system to work, but it's what we have and will need to deal with until Congress grows a spine to stop it. Given this judicial reality, the most important decisions for our children's and grandchildren's future is making sure solid, conservative legal minds are put on the high court who believe in limited government and constitutional checks and balances. Donald Trump has promised to do that.

Trump has said his model Supreme Court justice is the late, great Antonin Scalia. "Justice Scalia was a remarkable person and a brilliant Supreme Court Justice, one of the best of all time," Trump said upon receiving news that the justice had passed away. "His career was defined by his reverence for the Constitution and his legacy of protecting Americans' most cherished freedoms. He was a justice who did not believe in legislating from the bench, and he is a person whom I held in the highest regard and will always greatly respect his intelligence and conviction to uphold the Constitution of our country."[1]

In May 2016, Trump took the unprecedented step of releasing a list of eleven lawyers he might nominate to take Scalia's seat on the Supreme Court.[2] This list, which was compiled with the help of the conservative Heritage Foundation, the Federalist Society, the nation's leading organization of conservative lawyers, and Eagle Forum, includes the following top-notch candidates:[3]

- Steven Colloton of Iowa is a judge of the U.S. Court of Appeals for the Eighth Circuit, a position he has held since President George W. Bush appointed him in

2003. Judge Colloton has a résumé that also includes distinguished service as the U.S. Attorney for the Southern District of Iowa, a Special Assistant to the Attorney General in the Justice Department's Office of Legal Counsel, and a lecturer of law at the University of Iowa. He received his law degree from Yale, and he clerked for conservative Supreme Court Chief Justice William Rehnquist.

- Allison Eid of Colorado is an associate justice of the Colorado Supreme Court. Colorado Governor Bill Owens appointed her to the seat in 2006; she was later retained for a full term by the voters (with 75 percent of voters favoring retention). Prior to her judicial service, Justice Eid served as Colorado's solicitor general and as a law professor at the University of Colorado. Justice Eid attended the University of Chicago Law School, and she clerked for conservative Supreme Court Justice Clarence Thomas.

- Raymond Gruender of Missouri has been a judge of the U.S. Court of Appeals for the Eighth Circuit since his 2004 appointment by President George W. Bush. Judge Gruender, who sits in St. Louis, Missouri, has extensive prosecutorial experience, culminating with his time as the U.S. Attorney for the Eastern District of Missouri. Judge Gruender received a law degree and an M.B.A. from Washington University in St. Louis.

- Thomas Hardiman of Pennsylvania has been a judge of the U.S. Court of Appeals for the Third Circuit since 2007. Prior to serving as a circuit judge, he served as a judge of the U.S. District Court for the Western District of Pennsylvania since 2003. Before his judicial service, Judge Hardiman worked in private practice in Washington, D.C., and Pittsburgh. Judge Hardiman was the first in his family to attend college, graduating from Notre Dame.

- Raymond Kethledge of Michigan has been a judge of the U.S. Court of Appeals for the Sixth Circuit since 2008. Before his judicial service, Judge Kethledge served as judiciary counsel to

Michigan Republican Senator Spencer Abraham, worked as a partner in two law firms, and worked as an in-house counsel for the Ford Motor Company. Judge Kethledge obtained his law degree from the University of Michigan and clerked for Supreme Court Justice Anthony Kennedy.

- Joan Larsen of Michigan is an Associate Justice of the Michigan Supreme Court. Justice Larsen was a professor at the University of Michigan School of Law from 1998 until her appointment to the bench. In 2002, she temporarily left academia to work as an Assistant Attorney General in the Justice Department's Office of Legal Counsel. Justice Larsen received her law degree from Northwestern and clerked for the late conservative Supreme Court Justice Antonin Scalia.

- Thomas Lee of Utah has been an Associate Justice of the Utah Supreme Court since 2010. Beginning in 1997, he served on the faculty of Brigham Young University Law School, where he still teaches in an adjunct capacity. Justice Lee was

Deputy Assistant Attorney General in the Justice Department's Civil Division from 2004 to 2005. Justice Lee attended the University of Chicago Law School, and he clerked for conservative Supreme Court Justice Clarence Thomas. Justice Lee is also the son of former U.S. Solicitor General Rex Lee and the brother of current conservative Republican U.S. Senator Mike Lee.

- William H. Pryor Jr., of Alabama is a judge of the U.S. Court of Appeals for the Eleventh Circuit. He has served on the court since 2004. Judge Pryor became the Alabama Attorney General in 1997 upon Jeff Sessions' election to the U.S. Senate. Judge Pryor was then elected in his own right in 1998 and reelected in 2002. In 2013, Judge Pryor was confirmed to a term on the United States Sentencing Commission. Judge Pryor received his law degree from Tulane, and he clerked for Judge John Minor Wisdom of the U.S. Court of Appeals for the Fifth Circuit.

- David Stras of Minnesota has been an Associate Justice of the Minnesota

Supreme Court since 2010. After his initial appointment, he was elected to a six-year term in 2012. Prior to his judicial service, Judge Stras worked as a teacher at the University of Minnesota Law School. In his time there, he wrote extensively about the function and structure of the judiciary. Justice Stras received his law degree and an M.B.A. from the University of Kansas. He clerked for conservative Supreme Court Justice Clarence Thomas.

- Diane Sykes of Wisconsin has served as a judge of the U.S. Court of Appeals for the Seventh Circuit since 2004. Prior to her federal appointment, Judge Sykes had been a Justice of the Wisconsin Supreme Court since 1999 and a Wisconsin trial court judge of both civil and criminal matters before that. Judge Sykes received her law degree from Marquette.
- Don Willett of Texas has been a Justice of the Texas Supreme Court since 2005. He was initially appointed by Governor Rick Perry and has been reelected by the voters twice. Prior to his judicial

service, Judge Willett worked as a senior fellow at the Texas Public Policy Foundation, as an advisor in George W. Bush's gubernatorial and presidential administrations, as Deputy Assistant Attorney General in the Justice Department's Office of Legal Policy, and as a Deputy Attorney General under then-Texas Attorney General Greg Abbott. Justice Willett received his law degree and a master's degree from Duke.

Trump's pool of potential nominees to the Supreme Court received almost unanimous praise from intelligent conservatives. "We are encouraged by Mr. Trump's repeated pledges to appoint constitutionalists, which stands in sharp contrast to Hillary Clinton's position," said Marjorie Dannenfelser, a pro-life hero in Washington and president of the Susan B. Anthony List, which works to elect pro-life candidates to national office. "There is no question Clinton would only nominate judges who stand in lock-step with the abortion lobby and would strike down even the most modest abortion limits."[4]

At the Becket Fund for Religious Liberty, which has been fighting judicial activism under the Obama administration, senior counsel Hannah Smith, agreed.

"All of the potential nominees on the list have records of principled judicial philosophies and have demonstrated their commitment to interpreting the Constitution and laws as written, even under pressure," said Smith, who clerked for conservative justices Samuel Alito and Clarence Thomas. "[Trump's list of potential nominees] includes judges who take seriously the religious liberty of all Americans and who apply the law fairly to preserve this crucial constitutional right." The praise was echoed by the Judicial Action Network, whose chief counsel Carrie Severino said, "These are the kind of people [Senate Democrats] would block until the cows come home but I think it's a great list. If we could get the White House and keep the Senate, I think this would be an amazing opportunity to actually appoint someone who would be worthy to fill Justice Scalia's shoes."

It is vitally important that a Republican—and that means Donald Trump—appoint the next round of new Supreme Court justices. During the Obama presidency, the Court has defended creeping nationalized health through Obamacare and reinvented marriage to be open to two men or two women. Future cases could include landmark legal battles over immigration, abortion, gun rights, religious liberty, affirmative action, and presidential power.

Republican presidents do not have a good track record of appointing solid justices to the Supreme Court. It is to Trump's credit that his shortlist is as good as it is. He knows that America is at a crisis point. We need Supreme Court justices who will defend the Constitution and stand opposed, on firm judicial principle, to the Left's relentless attempts to legislate, and perpetuate a social (and socialist) revolution, from the bench.

"The Supreme Court has always been extremely important, on issues that belong in court such as the Second Amendment, Obamacare, and immigration," Breitbart News legal editor Ken Klukowski explained on Stephen K. Bannon's Sirius XM Patriot 125 radio show. "But conservatives have always understood that once the Supreme Court started in 1965 hijacking political issues that are not in the Constitution, such as abortion and marriage—overriding the will of the voters through judicial activism—that now if you have a liberal Supreme Court, the Court can shut down democracy anytime it wants by declaring something to be a constitutional issue…and so no issue is more important than a president's nominations for the High Court."[5] This is because the Court has seized power from the other two branches of government against the dictates of the Constitution, and no one has done anything about it. As constitutional scholar Larry Kramer explains:

In 1958, all nine justices signed an extraordinary opinion in *Cooper v. Aaron* insisting that *Marbury [v. Madison]* had "declared the basic principle that the federal judiciary is supreme in the exposition of the law of the Constitution" and that this idea "has ever since been respected by this Court and the country as permanent and indispensable feature of our constitutional system." This was, of course, just bluster and puff…*Marbury* said no such thing, and judicial supremacy was not cheerfully embraced in the years after *Marbury* was decided. The justices in *Cooper* were not reporting a fact so much as trying to manufacture one…The declaration of judicial interpretative supremacy evoked considerable skepticism at the time. But here is the striking thing: after *Cooper v. Aaron,* the idea of judicial supremacy seemed gradually, at long last, to find wide public acceptance.[6]

Since then, the Supreme Court has declared itself infinitely supreme, capable of knocking down or rewriting any law, with no check on its power. Acceptance of judicial supremacy means surrendering the principle of self-government.

The Heritage Foundation lists nine kinds of judicial activism through which "judges write subjective policy preferences into the law rather than apply the law impartially according to its original meaning." They include, abusing (or inventing) precedents, contorting the plain meaning of the constitution or laws, importing foreign law as if it were relevant, arbitrary decision-making that can only be called judicial dishonesty, judicial imperialism where the court assumes power and authority it does not have, nullifying rights, playing judicial favorites, regarding the constitution as a "living" document, and simply legislating from the bench.[7] All of which really means is that liberal justices on the Supreme Court do whatever the heck they want, unrestrained by law, precedent, the Constitution, reason, or logic, knowing as they do that no power will stop them—except a majority of justices appointed by Donald Trump.

The Founders designed the Supreme Court to be something very different from what it is today. "The court has, over the years, the activist judges have taken on a lot of things that the court was never supposed to be doing. They're supposed to be, simply look at the law, see if it comports to the Constitution," explains Carrie Severino, chief counsel and policy director for the Judicial Crisis Network, a grassroots conservative group that educates and organizes citizens to fight back against the encroaching power of the federal judiciary. "But when you have a court that is taking it upon itself to read new things into the Constitution, to say we think it's evolving and we're going to put our fingers to the wind and tell you which way we think society is going. That's not what the Court was designed for. That's what our elected branches were designed to do, to figure out how is society changing? How do we reflect that? The Court is simply there to make sure that those laws that the elected branches pass actually are being faithfully executed and make sure the Constitution is being stuck to."[8]

As Trump made clear with his shortlist of judicial candidates, he will appoint conservatives to the Supreme Court who understand that their limited role is simply to make sure the Constitution is being faithfully executed and not to re-engineer society as the progressive Left sees fit. Not only did he tell the authors of this book that his model Supreme Court justice is Antonin Scalia, he pledged to restore the proper constitutional balance to our federal government, working with Congress, rather than continuing Obama's lawless rule by executive order. Working with such rock-solid conservative advisers as Senator Jeff Sessions of Alabama and the Federalist Society, we believe that Donald Trump could finally, through his judicial appointments, restore the Supreme Court and the federal courts to their proper roles.

A vote for Donald Trump is a vote against judicial tyranny. And that's something every conservative should support.

CHAPTER 5

Education That Educates

How long do we think the United States can survive schools that pretend to teach while our kids only pretend to learn? How can a kid hope to build an American Dream when he hasn't been taught how to spell the word "dream"?

—Donald J. Trump

We've all read the news stories or seen the embarrassing videos posted on the Internet. A reporter at a school graduation saunters up to students, pokes a microphone in their face, and proceeds to ask completely basic questions about U.S. history that none of the gowned graduates can answer, even as they clutch their new diplomas. The litany of ignorance reveals a shocking lack of general knowledge among American students. Recent surveys of high-school graduates have shown that a majority cannot identify the century in which the U.S. Civil War occurred, list two of America's enemies in World War II, or name the Founder who wrote the Declaration of Independence. A recent sidewalk survey showed that most random people on the street can't even come up with who the nation's capital is named after. That Washington, D.C. is named after George Washington—our first president who was long known as the father of our country—is apparently too tricky for modern education to convey. This is a crisis of ignorance; and a scandal for a democracy.

The problem is too many diplomas aren't worth the paper they're printed on. In fact, while a record 82 percent of high schoolers graduated on time within four years in 2014, only 37 percent of these graduates were deemed ready for college-level reading and math courses, according to National Assessment of Educational Progress tests.[1] As Donald Trump has put it, "Our kids aren't learning. Too many are dropping out of school and into the street life—and too many of those who do graduate are getting diplomas that have been devalued into 'certificates of attendance' by a dumbed-down curriculum that asks little of teachers and less of students."[2] Dire statistics back up the GOP nominee's claim about exactly how bad a job America's schools are doing at teaching American kids what they need to learn to succeed in the competitive, modern world. And even worse, these numbers continue to decline. Math scores fell two points in 2015 from

2014, and reading proficiency has dropped five points since the 1990s.

Money is not and has never been the problem. "The American educational system is failing. We're 26th in the world—26th!" Trump wrote with frustration in 2015. "We spend more money on education, per capita, than any other nation—but 25 countries in the developed world provide a better education for their kids than we do for ours."[3] It's sadly symbolic that some of the worst schools in the country are in our capital, where the public-school system is lavishly funded. Despite spending an astounding $30,000 per student, 81 percent of the eighth-grade students in D.C. schools are not proficient in math, and 83 percent are not proficient at reading.[4] Many of these students graduate from high school with no more than basic elementary-school skills and knowledge. Of those graduates who go to college, many are unprepared for college level work—even as that college-level has been dumbed down. According to Education Reform Now, 25 percent of university freshmen are required to enroll in remedial classes during their first year in college to catch up on basic skills they should have but did not learn in high school.[5] This is an expensive bill added on top of the already high expense of a college education as the remedial courses are estimated to cost students a whopping $1.5 billion per year. That tab does not include the additional fees and expenses that accrue because graduation is delayed and tuition and fees paid for additional semesters as students must pay to get up to speed before they can begin normal college classes. On average, remedial students take one full extra year to graduate from college, adding between $14,120 and $26,400 to the total cost of their education. That's if they even graduate. Students who take remedial classes are 74 percent more likely to drop out of college.

"These students [who need to take remedial classes in college] face such drastically higher odds of never getting a degree," reflected Mary Nguyen Barry, one of the authors of the study by Education Reform Now. "And if you end up degreeless with debt, you don't have the benefits of added earning power, and you're four times more likely to default on your student loans."

The disaster that is the American education system affects children from families at all income levels. According to the Education Reform Now report, 45 percent of remedial students are from middle- and upper-income backgrounds. "People are underestimating the breadth and depth of high-school underperformance," co-author Michael Dannenberg told the *Washington Post*. "They think it's not their kids."

Not much progress has been made on addressing this problem in the last twenty years. In 2000, the percentage of American university students who needed to take remedial classes their first year in college was 30 percent. Trump was ahead of the curve on this subject and talked about the costs of underperforming schools at length at the turn of millennium:

> About a third of our students are going to college to learn what they should have learned in high school. Parents and taxpayers are paying once in high school, once in college to educate kids in the basics. They're getting fleeced. Nor is remedial education going to save us. We're doing worse than treading water; we're going under. According to school-testing experts' rule of thumb, the average child's achievement score *declines* about 1% for each year they're in school. That gives the expression "dumbing down" a whole new meaning. Schools may be hazardous to your child's intellectual health.[6]

Trump's main solution for failing schools was the same in 2000 as it is now: more competition. Trump has been talking about the need for greater school choice for decades. "Competition is why I'm very much in favor of school choice. Let schools compete for kids," Trump said in 2015. "I guarantee that if you forced schools to get better or close because parents didn't want to enroll their kids there, they would get better. Competition makes you stronger, it forces you to work harder, to do more."[7] His tune has been the same for three decades. "Our public schools have grown up in a competition-free zone, surrounded by a very high union wall. We've got to bring on the competition—open the schoolhouse doors and let parents choose the best school for their children," Trump argued seventeen years ago. "In an environment where there's competition and choice, there's a constant effort to offer quality at competitive cost."[8]

"When teachers' unions say even the most miniscule program allowing school choice is a mortal threat, they're saying: If we aren't allowed to keep 90 percent of the market, we can't survive," remarks Trump. "When Bell Telephone had 90 percent of the market, a federal judge broke it up." As the Republican nominee proposes, it is past time to break up this monopoly in public education.

Donald Trump believes that parents deserve more say in how their children are educated. "The federal Department of Education has been dictating educational policy for too long, and that needs to stop. Common Core doesn't work," Trump says. "We should return the basic control and responsibility for our schools to the states and local communities. They need to set standards for their teachers and students that reward competition and excellence."

Trump has six key principles for reforming education: a back to basics approach with old school standards of knowledge and grading; a focus on real results ("Forget that self-esteem stuff; we need to start challenging kids," Trump says); a restoration of school discipline; merit pay (rather than pay by seniority) for teachers; vastly improved civic education so that children know far more about American history; and expanding school choice so that schools can innovate free from bureaucratic mandates to offer the best education possible for the children of the families they serve.[9]

Astoundingly, the Republican Congress actually gave President Obama *more* authority over the nation's schools by passing school reform legislation that included the poison pill that state and local education programs had to be approved by the U.S. Department of Education. For the past fifty years, the engine of federal control over local schools has been Title I of the Elementary and Secondary Education Act (ESEA) of 1965. It was the first in a series of socialist laws that President Lyndon Johnson promised would lead to a "Great Society." Johnson's Great Society legislation was speedily enacted by a Congress in which Democrats outnumbered Republicans by more than two to one (295 to 140 in the House and 68 to 32 in the Senate). Despite the trillions of dollars spent since 1965, we're no closer to achieving a Great Society; by many measures, America's education and social welfare are much worse today than when those programs were launched fifty years ago.

Republicans had an opportunity to dismantle the failed regime of federal control when they regained control of both Houses of Congress in 1994 and then elected a president in 2000. Unfortunately, The Republicans' big idea was No Child Left Behind (NCLB), which promised to bring all children to 100 percent proficiency in basic skills by 2014. That was an admirable goal, but of course it didn't happen, and nearly everyone now recognizes NCLB as a complete failure. Somehow Republicans in Congress cannot seem to act on the most fundamental conservative principle of education reform, which is to dismantle the federal education bureaucracy entirely, and to trim it back at the state and local level, returning power to parents. Instead, congressional Republicans continue to push for Federal solutions, as with the "Every Student Succeeds Act," which President Obama gladly signed at the end of 2015.

It has been astonishing to us that so many pundits and politicians have claimed that Donald Trump is not a reliable conservative, when on issue after issue, including most especially education reform, he has consistently supported much more conservative solutions than the self-styled defenders of conservative orthodoxy, who in many cases simply slightly modify what liberals believe, whether it is the free trade dogma of Barack Obama and Hillary Clinton, or an education reform bill like the Every Student Succeeds Act which was coauthored by liberal Washington Democrat Senator Patty Murray and supported by the liberal National Education Association, teachers' unions, and President Obama.

In 1988, the last year of his presidency, Ronald Reagan paraphrased William Bennett, his secretary of education, about the crisis in our nation's schools. "If you serve a child a rotten hamburger in America, federal, state, and local agencies will investigate you, summon you, close you down, whatever," the Gipper explained. "But if you provide a child with a rotten education, nothing happens, except that you're likely to be given more money to do it with. Well, we've discovered that money alone isn't the answer."[10] Reagan had wanted to abolish the Department of Education and institute school vouchers for school choice, but was foiled by the education bureaucracy and Congress. Today, the budget for the U.S. Department of Education is $77.4 billion.[11] In 1980, the federal education budget was $14 billion.[12] Conservatives have lost the fight to diminish the federal role in education big-time, partly because Republicans have themselves pushed for greater federal funding because they think it proves they're pro-education. Now with Donald Trump we finally have a Republican presidential nominee who wants to get the feds out of the classroom—and has made that issue a priority of his campaign. In his speech at Trump Tower announcing his candidacy, Trump boldly declared that "Common Core is a disaster. Education has to be local."

On the issue of education reform, Trump might even succeed where Reagan failed. Trump has told the authors of this book that he intends to kill Common Core and eliminate education bureaucracies that stifle innovation and effective teaching. He intends to bring a results-oriented business mindset to education, drastically reducing the role of the federal government so that bureaucrats make fewer decisions and parents get to make more. "Education has to be run locally. Common Core, No Child Left Behind, and Race to the Top are all programs that take decisions away from parents and local school boards," Trump says. "These programs allow the progressives in the Department of Education to indoctrinate, not educate, our kids. What they are doing does not fit the American model of governance. I am totally against these programs and the Department of Education."[13] *This* is a conservative vision, it is Trump's vision, and it is yet one more reason why conservatives should vote to put Donald Trump in the White House.

CHAPTER 6

A Family Man

The happiest people I know are those people who have great families and real values. People who have a loving spouse and have children they really love are happy people.

—Donald J. Trump

Donald Trump has dedicated all of his fifteen bestselling books to his parents. He has said over and over again that they made him who he is, but for different reasons. His mother and father provided very different advice, but he honored what both of them told him to do. "My mother was a wife who really was a great homemaker. She always said, 'Be happy!'" Trump recalls. "My father said, 'I want you to be successful.' He was a very driven kind of guy that pushed me pretty hard. My father was a tough man but a good man. He would tell me to always do something that you love."[1] Trump explains it was this family support—a full time homemaker mother and an ambitious hard-working father—that gave him the confidence to take risks to strive toward his dream and ultimately become successful.

In tough times, Trump focuses on his family. Trump is a famous celebrity known for his brash manner and tough-guy image, but it's his children and wife that provide the support he needs to face the world and stare down the tough times. "Anyone who visits my office will notice that I have many photographs of my family—my parents, my children, and Melania. That's a great positive focus to keep, not that I need reminders, but a glance now and then can keep things in perspective," Trump explains. "I also have photos and mementos of achievements that have meant a lot to me over the years—so that if the going is rough, I have tangible reminders of past successes. None of them were easy either."[2]

Critics can, and will, go on and on about Trump having been married three times, and about how, in the past, he boasted about his indiscretions. But anyone who meets him today will meet an old-fashioned man grounded in his two great priorities—hard work and family—and a man who in other respects has led a remarkably clean life: "I've never taken drugs of any kind, never had a glass of alcohol. Never had a cigarette, never had a cup of coffee," Trump says. This "straight-edge" living is remarkable especially for a man of such wealth and success.

His five children and his wife Melania are his closest advisors and defenders. Trump credits his wife,
who he brags is "a very smart woman" with "amazing
instincts," for encouraging him to run for president in
2016. He speaks like a husband who loves and respects
his wife AND who listens to her advice!

"For years, I would ask her whether or not I could
run and win. And she would say, 'Donald, people love
you, but they wouldn't vote for you for president.'
When I asked her why, she said, 'You're a little wild and
a little too controversial. They respect you, they think
you're smart—but enough people just wouldn't vote for
you,'" he recalls. "So she told me this for a long period
of time and then recently, as she's watching political
news on television and seeing all the things that are
wrong with our country, she looks at me and says,
'Darling, you know you'd win if you ran, don't you?'"
The challenges facing America and the mood of the
country had changed Melania's mind, and she changed
his. "Now you could win, and maybe even easily. People really want you," she explained. "I see it on the
streets. People want you and they really need you."[3]

A RESILIENT LEADER

Trump knows success is not a one way street, and
he, like any successful businessman or leader, learns

from his mistakes. "Understand that difficulties, mistakes, and setbacks are an inevitable part of business and life. Don't allow problems to knock you off your feet," he advises. "Learn from each situation. As you deal with each problem, note what you learned and don't repeat that same mistake."[4]

That's been true of his family life as well. "Truthfully, I was a much better father than I was a husband, always working too much to be the husband my wives wanted me to be. I blame myself," Trump admitted in 2015. "I was making my mark in the real estate business, and it was very hard for a relationship to compete with that aspect of my life."[5] He commented on these personal failures at more length in 2000, when there was a movement to enlist Trump to run against establishment politicians Al Gore and George W. Bush for the presidency. "I haven't been as successful in my marriages as my parents were, but marriage is not the only family value that matters," he said. "The importance you give to your relationship with your kids is a family value. So is your relationship with your parents, your sisters and brothers..."[6] And after two failed attempts at marriage—though he remains on good terms with both his ex-wives—he seems to have found success with his wife Melania; by all appearances, they are extremely happily married.

Moreover, Trump seems to have a terrific relationship with his children. No less an authority than pediatrician, and best-selling author, Meg Meeker has noted that "No matter what we think of him as a presidential candidate, he really appears to be a great dad."[7]

His loyalty to family extends to his friends, his associates, and most especially his country. "Loyalty is a version of your love for your family," Trump says. "I feel loyalty not only to my friends but also to my city and to my country. By my definition, one of my family values is patriotism." Edmund Burke, the founder of modern conservatism, couldn't have said it better.

FAITH

Christianity is under attack around the world—most dramatically from Islamists, but also insidiously here at home with attacks on religious freedom. Donald Trump has made a point about speaking out against the persecution of Christians abroad and against the Left's political correctness that is trying to ban public expressions of Christianity at home. "I'm proud to be a Christian," Donald Trump has said, "and as president I will not allow Christianity to be consistently attacked and weakened, unlike what is happening now with our current president."

As with family, Trump notes that "religion plays a very large factor in happiness. People who have God in their lives receive a tremendous amount of joy and satisfaction from their faith." Of his own religious background, he has volunteered that he grew up going to Sunday school Bible class every week at the First Presbyterian Church in Jamaica, Queens, New York City, and as an adult learned a lot about spirituality and the inner strength that comes from it by getting to know Norman Vincent Peale and attending his church. "The church had a strong influence on me. I think people are shocked when they find out that I am a Christian, that I am a religious person," Trump admits. "I go to church, I love God, and I love having a relationship with Him. I am who I am, and deep down, the Gospels helped make me that person."[8] His earnestness in expressing his simple, personal faith is partly why he won such strong support from evangelical voters in the Republican primaries.

RELIGIOUS LIBERTY

The importance Trump puts on personal faith inspires Trump to be vigilant against threats to the religious freedom of others. He has boldly asserted that when he is president, people will feel free to say "Merry Christmas" again. This is not merely an off-the-cuff applause line for religiously conservative campaign crowds but reflects his long-term thinking about the dangers of public pressure to suppress religious expression and sentiment. "It seems like every week there is a negative ruling on some issue having to do with Christians…The fact is that our deep-rooted religious beliefs have made this country great. That belief in the lessons of the Bible has had a lot to do with our growth and success," Trump says. He laments that there are now "restrictions on what you can put up in a beautiful public area. Mary and the baby Jesus are seldom shown, and even the word 'Christmas' has somehow become controversial. Who in the world could be offended by someone saying 'Merry Christmas'?! It's a wonderful tradition." On the campaign trail, he says frequently that Christians need to quit being the "silent" majority and stand up for their beliefs.

Trump is also outspoken on the need to defend Christians in Muslim countries, and other countries where they are persecuted. "So you tell me about religious liberty and freedom. The Christians are being treated horribly because we have nobody to represent the Christians," he said about the genocide of Christians by the Islamic State in Syria and the Obama administration's refusal to do anything to stop the slaughter. "Believe me, if I run and I win, I will be the greatest representative of the Christians they've had in a long time."[9]

ABORTION

Trump has gone to great lengths to court national leaders in the social-conservative movement and has convinced many of the most prominent ones that he genuinely supports their policy positions. Ralph Reed, founder of the Faith and Freedom Coalition and former longtime spokesman for the Christian Coalition, says, "On social and moral issues—marriage, abortion, religious liberty, support for Israel—Trump not only checks all those boxes, but if you go to one of his rallies, it's surprising how much of his stump speech speaks to those issues."[10]

Trump's credentials as a pro-life advocate are at least as good as Mitt Romney's, in fact, arguably they're better. Back in 2011, Trump stated, "There are certain things that I don't think can ever be negotiated. Let me put it this way: I am pro-life, and pro-life people will find out that I will be very loyal to them, just as I am loyal to other people. I would be appointing judges that feel the way I feel."[11]

While he has expressed ambivalence about Planned Parenthood as an institution, he has shown no ambivalence about criticizing Planned Parenthood's abortion clinics and promising to slash their federal funding. In 2015 he said flatly, "I am against abortion," and lambasted Planned Parenthood's large-scale involvement in the abortion business.[12]

He has supported pro-life legislation. "A ban on elective abortions after twenty weeks will protect unborn children," Trump said about the Pain-Capable Unborn Child Protection Act in 2011. "We should not be one of seven countries that allows elective abortions after twenty weeks. It goes against our core values."[13]

Trump became pro-life, in the words of author George Beahm, when abortion "ceased to be an abstract concept and became personalized." Or as Trump has said, "I'm pro-life, but I changed my view a number of years ago. One of the reasons I changed...A friend of mine's wife was pregnant and he didn't want the baby. He ends up having the baby and the baby is the apple of his eye. It's the greatest thing that has ever happened to him. And you know, here's a baby that wasn't going to be let into life. I heard this, and some other stories, and I'm pro-life. The stories changed me."[14] A man who can have that sort of heartfelt conversion is a good man.

And Trump has made clear he understands how to fight abortion: "I will protect it and the biggest way to protect it is through the Supreme Court and putting people in the court…I will appoint Supreme Court judges who will be pro-life."[15]

THE REAGAN MODEL

Ralph Reed says that religious voters vote on the same issues as everyone else, but place them within a spiritual context. If Christians voted primarily on Christian identity, he notes, "They would not have voted for Ronald Reagan, the first divorced man who was ever elected president, over [Democrat] Jimmy Carter, who was a very pious Southern Baptist. He was a member of their denomination, many of them, yet they voted for Reagan," Reed says. But religious voters saw then that the divorced and remarried Ronald Reagan better represented their political beliefs than the hapless Jimmy Carter, and even had a better understanding of the moral, social, and cultural—at bottom, religious—challenges facing our country.

For religious and pro-family voters, Donald Trump is without a doubt the best presidential option we've had in a long time—not someone who will take religious voters for granted (as so many GOP candidates have done), not someone who will try to buy us off with empty promises (ditto), not someone who will give our concerns low priority, but someone who keenly, personally, believes in defending public Christianity and fighting for the pro-life cause by supporting legislative restrictions on abortion and appointing pro-life Supreme Court justices. Donald Trump deserves the vote of every pro-life, pro-religious freedom conservative.

CHAPTER 7

Petty Tyranny

We're going to get rid of all these ridiculous regulations that are destroying us. You can't breathe.

—Donald J. Trump

There are two kinds of petty tyranny imposed by the Left. The first is political correctness—which strikes directly at the first principles of freedom of speech and freedom of conscience, which we've talked about.

The second is stifling red tape, regulation, and bureaucratic rules and edicts—all based on the theory that bureaucrats (especially federal bureaucrats) know best.

No politician that we can think of is better positioned and has more motivation to roll back job-killing red tape than Donald J. Trump.

THE TYRANNY OF REGULATION

Regulation is a major enforcer of the Left's agenda. The Left knows that regardless of elections, they can get their way by imposing regulations inch-by-inch (or, given their preference for the metric system, maybe we should say centimeter-by-centimeter) while the establishment stands by, clueless as to what's happening. The Democrat Party, which once rallied under the banner of getting the government out of your bedroom has since inserted Uncle Sam not only into your bedroom, but into your bathroom, laundry room, closet, kitchen, and garage. No aspect of our lives is too insignificant to come under the scrutiny of the federal government.

No toilet, dishwasher, shower head, light bulb, or washing machine may be sold without the consent of bureaucrats in Washington. Not surprisingly, devices bearing the federal government's seal of approval aren't better, they're demonstrably worse. For instance:

- Red-light cameras, encouraged by federal grants and propaganda, are replacing cops on America's streets, and the change is costing lives.

- Incandescent bulbs, now banned, were popular because they were cheap, effective, and safe. If you dropped one, you swept up the glass and threw it in the trash. Now if you drop one of the fluorescent fixtures the Democrats have foisted on us, you need to call a hazardous material team to clean up the toxic mess.

- Blue-gloved Transportation Safety Administration minions now harass millions of airline travelers in the name of security—at a cost of $8 billion a year, exceedingly long lines, and pointless, invasive, humiliating searches—yet they haven't stopped a single terrorist, or even managed to spot the terrorist watch list employees in their own ranks.

Americans are supposed to love freedom, but never in our nation's history have we been so bossed around by leftist bureaucrats and their endless regulations—a rolling tide of red tape that the Republican Congress has not only failed to stem but actually extended, because Republicans politicians like to say that they too can regulate in the so-called public interest.

Donald Trump, we believe, will be different, because Donald Trump is not a career politician; he is a businessman who has had to navigate Washington's shoals of red tape. As he says bluntly, "Government at all levels has saddled businessmen and women with ridiculous, dream-killing regulations."[1]

He intends to stop that.

He's going to do more than just talk about the problem—he's going to do something about it. "Blaming bureaucrats is easy," he says. "Every election has hundreds of candidates who bash the bureaucracy. When they take office, lo and behold, they discover that the bureaucrats are more powerful than they thought. Or it becomes clear that playing along with bureaucrats can be personally very rewarding,"[2] because every new regulation comes with powerful lobbyists and special interest backers; and politicians can wrap every new regulation with an aura of good intentions, even after they prove to be burdensome, job-killing, and full of unintended negative consequences. As Trump says:

> I know that the defenders of these policies are saying, "We meant well." But the time is long past for us, as a nation, to accept the "good intentions" dodge when major mistakes have been committed. In real life,

intentions really don't matter—results are what count. And we know what works and what doesn't. We should have a zero-tolerance policy for people who advocate discredited regulatory schemes. They had their chance, and they produced a debacle. In my opinion, these people are opportunity destroyers. They're guilty of what I call Dreamicide.[3]

Donald Trump has lived the American Dream. He wants to make that dream real for others by liberating entrepreneurs from the shackles of government regulation so that these practical dreamers can create new businesses, new jobs, and more prosperity.

The late, great political columnist Robert Novak used to warn that while Republicans in Washington fought for smaller government programs, all those small government programs still added up to really big government, which was why even when they "succeeded," Republicans lost the battle against big government.

Big government is popular with politicians, Novak noted, but he was skeptical that voters really liked it. "The notion that the American people want all this government but that they just don't want to pay for it is the biggest canard foisted on us by today's politicians and media." It was a self-serving justification for Republicans for why they had to capitulate to more government spending and regulation.

"What the country needs," Novak said, "is a leader, and a leader who will make his first priority speaking over the heads of the Beltway types to say, 'No more. Let's really cut government down to size.'"[4] That meant taking on the special interests, something that even conservatives had a hard time doing. "Well-meaning conservatives," Novak lamented, "get caught up in procuring the benefits of the federal leviathan for their states and their constituents."[5]

Donald Trump, however, is a different sort of politician. He isn't owned by special interests; he has no need to serve them; and his business career has shown him how damaging red tape can be. "What has brought us low is government bureaucracy and corruption," says Trump. An America with fewer bureaucrats and more businessmen and businesswomen will be a better America, an America on the road to being great again.

THE CAN-DO CANDIDATE

Donald Trump often tells the story of how he took over the project of renovating the Wollman Skating Rink—a project the City of New York could never complete, not in six years and twelve million dollars over budget, and that had become an eyesore. Trump told the city, "Just give the project to me. I'll finish the rink by Christmas. This Christmas. And I'll do it for free."

And he did, completing the renovation two months ahead of schedule, and $750,000 under budget, and turned it into an immediate money-maker (he donated the profits to charity).

That's the sort of can-do spirit—and record—that comes with Donald Trump. He will not be stifled by bureaucrats. He will not accept bureaucratic delays and overruns. He will get things done.

In that spirit, the spirit of a can-do businessman, no politician since Ronald Reagan has been more committed to slashing red tape and government bureaucracy than Donald Trump. No presidential candidate since Reagan has come to the task with more of a can-do attitude than Trump. And no president of the United States is more likely to successfully shame Republican congressmen into actually living up to their anti-big government rhetoric than Donald Trump. He will have no fear of telling do-nothing Republican chairmen of Senate and House committees, "You're fired!" and forming alliances with true conservatives equally committed to getting things done.

To fight the petty tyranny of federal bureaucrats, to repeal the red tape that kills jobs, we need Donald Trump in the White House.

CHAPTER 8

Military Superiority

Our military dominance must be unquestioned.

—Donald J. Trump

America is a nation at war. Whether a president who sympathizes with Islam acknowledges it or not, a large chunk of the Muslim world is actively engaged in undermining our way or life or supporting jihadist organizations planning terrorist attacks on our soil. Across the Pacific Ocean, which used to be under the unchallenged command of the U.S. 7th Fleet, the Communist People's Republic of China is undertaking a feverish military buildup and daily violating the territorial integrity of American allies, while we do nothing in response. North Korea has nuclear weapons; Iran will soon have its own nukes; and Russia, a power that then-secretary of State Hillary Clinton hoped to conciliate with a "reset" of American-Russian relations, has instead become a stronger potential enemy. Russian and Chinese fighters have buzzed American vessels and harassed our planes in the air. Libya (which had sworn off terrorism during the presidency of George W. Bush) is now a disaster; and ISIS is today more powerful as a terrorist organization than al-Qaeda was at its height. After eight years of Obama, the world is a much more dangerous place, and America is viewed as a nation in decline. Donald Trump wants to make American great again—and that means vastly improving our national defense so that no country in the world can, or would want to, threaten us. Aggressive nations make war, President Reagan once said, when they "believe the price of aggression is cheap."[1] An overwhelmingly strong U.S. military is still the best deterrent to any hostile actor on the world stage. Unfortunately, under President Obama and former secretary of State Hillary Clinton, our military has taken a whipping from political correctness, endured savage budget cuts, and been saddled with an incoherent national strategy.

UNDERMINING FROM WITHIN

Obama and Hillary Clinton take the left-wing view of America and American history—that America is a

country tarred by racism and sexism and nationalism
that needs to be taken down a peg or two for a more
just and egalitarian world order. They believe in
appeasing radical Islam rather than confronting it.
They believe in weakening American power so that
we don't "impose our values on others" (though
they're quite happy to impose leftist ideas where they
can). And they want to transform the United States
military from America's war-fighting machine into
another federally controlled bureaucracy where they
can push their politically correct social agendas.

To this end, the Obama administration has instituted political correctness where it may be the most
dangerous—in how we protect ourselves from *Islamist
terrorism*, a phrase the administration can't even
utter.

National security reporter Patrick Poole noted that
at the direction of the White House, anti-terrorism
trainers and training, including at the FBI, the Department of Homeland Security, and the Defense Department, were censored "on the basis of whether certain
Muslim groups...deemed them offensive." Some of
these Muslim groups, he reported, have "highly ques-
tionable records" yet they have been allowed to institute "a fundamental transformation of how our
nation's national security, intelligence, and law-
enforcement agencies conduct counter-terrorism."[2] It

has also led to the canceling of anti-terrorism seminars (because of alleged anti-Islamic bias), limits on what analysts can say or investigate (they are not allowed to link "mainstream" Muslim organizations with terror), and bureaucratic speech codes. Notoriously, the Obama administration officially prohibits the use of the phrase "Islamic terrorism" (and similar phrases) and even went to the absurd extent of initially redacting from law enforcement transcripts the words of the terrorist shooter in Orlando whenever he mentioned his adherence to Islamist groups or individuals. The Obama administration—and the Left in general—literally cannot confront the truth about Islamist terror.

The Obama administration is more worried about so-called "Islamophobia" than it is about Islamist terrorists. In fact, the Pentagon and the State Department under Hillary Clinton sent stern warnings to its employees about any activity that might be construed as anti-Muslim. The FBI actually purged its criminal library, records, official presentations, and training materials of thousands of documents due to complaints that its counter-terrorism operations were "intolerant." With these "see no evil, hear no evil, speak no evil" policies in place, it's hardly surprising that at least seventy-three jihadists on terrorist watch lists were employed at Homeland Security itself, and that the department has partnered with groups identified by the Justice Department as having terror-ist connections.[3]

This blinding of America's intelligence apparatus was responsible for the FBI ignoring clues that could have prevented the refugees-turned-terrorists from perpetrating the Boston Marathon bombing, and helps explain why so many red flags were ignored about the Orlando jihadist Omar Mateen who was not shy about loudly proclaiming Islamist views.[4] The Obama administration likes to trumpet the nursery-rhyme-like slogan, "See something, say something," but many people—such as gun-store clerks and wait-resses—reported suspicious activity by Mateen and his wife Noor Salman and it was ignored. Libertarian journalist Liz Sheld wryly reflected that the terrorists would have gotten more attention from federal author-ities if a store owner would have refused to sell them a same-sex wedding cake instead of body armor and ammunition.[5] This dereliction of duty is not a case of overlooking signs but the deliberate averting of eyes by officials badgered into being politically correct and putting the sensitivity of Muslims over the safety of innocents. The willful abandonment of a serious focus on national security has enabled eighty-six acts of Islamic terrorism since 9/11, including twenty-two plots since the beginning of 2015 and six in 2016 preceding the Orlando attack in June.[6]

According to Daniel Pipes, an expert on the Islamist threat, "Jihadi violence in the West increased 50 percent a year since 2012, [and there are likely] many more increases ahead."[7] We need a giant redirection of American policy to confront the threat posed by radical Islam. That's something we won't get from Hillary Clinton. It's something we manifestly will get from Donald Trump.

INSANE ASYLUM

After the jihadist attack in Orlando, Donald Trump said of Obama's reaction, "We're led by a man that either is not tough, not smart, or he's got something else in mind. There's something going on."[8] Count us among those who think something else is going on. Obama referred to "my Muslim faith" on *ABC News* in 2008, something which doesn't easily slip off the average tongue. And although the episode has been largely covered up in recent years, Obama proudly recited the Muslim morning call to prayer in Arabic during his first presidential run, which *New York Times* reporter Nicholas Kristof noted was "with a first-rate accent."[9] In 2010, it was reported that President Obama had instructed the head of NASA to make as his "foremost" priority "to find a way to reach out to the Muslim world and engage much more with dominantly Muslim nations to help them feel good about their historic contribution to science, math, and engineering."[10] Sorry, but that is not normal, even from a liberal Democrat president, and neither are his policies toward welcoming in hordes of unscreened Muslims from terrorist-sponsoring lands.

According to data from the Department of Homeland Security, by the time he leaves office, Obama will have given more than *one million* green cards to immigrants from Muslim-majority countries. The FBI has admitted there is no way to safely vet these people because reliable documents identifying who they are and what connections they have often simply do not exist.[11] "We can only query against that which we have collected," FBI Director James Comey testified to the House Committee on Homeland Security in October 2015. "So if someone has never made a ripple in the pond in Syria in a way that would get their identity or their interest reflected in our database, we can query our database until the cows come home, but... nothing [will] show up because we have no record of them."[12] Bringing in so many unvetted Muslims makes zero sense when the civilized world is locked in a struggle against Islamist terrorism.

Breitbart News reported that in the first six fiscal years of Obama's presidency, the administration granted "832,014 green cards to migrants from majority-Muslim countries." Most "were issued to migrants from Pakistan (102,000), Iraq (102,000), Bangladesh (90,000), Iran (85,000), Egypt (56,000), and Somalia (37,000)."[13] Not counted in these numbers are people entering the country on temporary student, work, or tourist visas, who commonly stay after their visas expire. The media tripped over themselves to trumpet that the Orlando shooter was born in America, as if that somehow negated the Islamic inspiration for his terrorist attack. But as Trump pointed out, the terrorist's parents were from Afghanistan, and if they hadn't been admitted from that Islamist state, their mass murderer son, who proclaimed his allegiance to radical Islam over the United States, wouldn't have been here.[14] That is a simple and logical connecting of the dots.[15]

Another bizarre twist to Obama's asylum and immigration policies is that those he's bringing in skew overwhelmingly Muslim at a time when ISIS is actively conducting genocide against Christians in the Middle East. Approximately 18 percent of Syrian refugees are Christian, but only 3 percent of the almost 2,200 brought to America by the Obama administration between 2011 and 2015 were Christian.[16] Of the five hundred Syrian refugees imported to the United States in the first three weeks of May 2016, none were Christian, all were Muslim. In the first eight months of the 2016 fiscal year, 0.44 percent of the refugees were Christian.[17]

If this immigration program is genuinely for compassionate, humanitarian reasons, why isn't the United States helping more Christians escape slaughter at the hands of the Islamic fanatics? Instead, the federal government is importing Muslims from ISIS-dominated areas that security officials admit they cannot vet. Making matters worse, Hillary wants a five hundred percent increase in Muslim refugees over Obama's program.[18] Al-Qaeda or ISIS couldn't have cooked up a better game plan for spreading jihad here.

"What has happened in Orlando is just the beginning. Our leadership is weak and ineffective," Trump said the day after the terrorist attack. He reiterated his call for a temporary ban on immigrants from countries linked to Islamic terror, saying that if we're going to protect innocent American lives, we can't be politically correct; we "must be tough."[19]

Especially given the experience of Europe—where Islamic immigration and "refugees" have been linked to a litany of sexual assaults that have been directly tied to Islamic "culture"[20]—you would think that anyone concerned about the safety of American citizens would not be importing potential Islamist violence to our neighborhoods.

Unfortunately, it's not just left-wingers like Hillary Clinton and Barack Obama pushing the happy-clappy line that Islam is a religion of peace; even some Republican leaders are pretending unvetted Muslims from radicalized parts of the world pose no possible threat.

House Speaker Paul Ryan threatened that he would sue a President Trump, the leader of his own party, to stop any ban on Muslims entering the country. When asked by the *Huffington Post* about Trump's proposed temporary ban on immigrants from radical Islamic countries, Ryan insisted, "I would sue any president that exceeds his or her powers."[21] That raises the interesting question of why Ryan hasn't sued Obama for his repeated overreaches of executive authority. The fact is, the United States is under no obligation to take any and all refugees or immigrants; Obama threw open the gates; Trump can close them again. That's called national sovereignty.

During Obama's presidency, Muslim immigration has become the fastest-growing source of new immigrants. Yet for the most part, these people are not bringing skills or knowledge that are in demand here, and most go onto the public dole immediately. According to the Office of Refugee Resettlement, 91 percent of immigrants from the Middle East get food stamps, 73 percent receive Medicaid or other taxpayer-funded health-care benefits, and 68 percent are handed cash welfare payments.[22] Many of these immigrants come to the United States believing in sharia law, and some, like the father of terrorist Omar Mateen, might be supporters of the Taliban; we have no way of knowing for sure.[23] So why exactly are we bringing these people to the United States?

Barack Obama's Middle East refugee program is bad; Hillary's is worse. As Trump says, "under the Clinton plan, you'd be admitting hundreds of thousands of refugees from the Middle East with no system to vet them, or to prevent the radicalization of their children."[24] Why is this in the interest of the United States? Answer: it isn't, but few politicians aside from Donald Trump are willing to say so, and are pledged to do something about it. If you want a vitally important reason to vote for Donald Trump, this is it.

CHRONICLE OF DECLINE

Here's another reason: we live in an obviously dangerous world, face an international ideological threat in the shape of Islamist terror, and confront potentially aggressive Communist nuclear powers like North Korea and China. Yet our Army is now smaller than it was in 1940,[25] and America military power is declining rapidly. Taking 1991 as our starting point (after victory in the Cold War and the First Gulf War):[26]

- Our active duty armed forces have shrunk from 2 million to about 1.3 million.
- Our Navy has been cut from more than 500 ships to only 272.
- The Air Force is about 1/3 smaller, and our combat fleet of B-52s is more than twice as old as the airmen in the cockpits.

Moreover:

- America's once powerful nuclear arsenal is so antiquated that the launching mechanisms are based on machines made fifty years ago. "The command-and-control system, which coordinates the operational functions of the United States nuclear forces, [including] intercontinental ballistic missiles, nuclear bombers, and tanker-support aircraft runs on an IBM Series/1 computer—a 1970s computing system—and uses 8-inch floppy disks," according to the Government Accountability Office.[27]

- President Obama has proposed a 2017 defense budget that cuts nearly 25 percent from what the United States was spending a mere five years ago.

It's time to do something about this military degradation before it's too late. "We will spend what we need to rebuild our military. We will develop, build and purchase the best equipment known to mankind," Trump vows. "Our military dominance must be unquestioned." And our national defense priority will be what it should be: defending America. As Senator Jeff Sessions, one of the most reliable conservatives in Congress and a close Trump advisor, explains, "We're going to defeat the people who are direct threats to us, but we're going to be a lot more cautious about getting involved in long-term, Wilsonian adventures."[28]

Trump believes it's time for a new foreign policy that addresses today's threats. Trump believes that "After the Cold War, our foreign policy veered badly off course. We failed to develop a new vision for a new time. It all began with the dangerous idea that we could make Western democracies out of countries that had no experience or interest in becoming a Western Democracy." Our foreign policy, he says, needs to go back to the basics with a more clear-eyed vision of what is truly in America's national interests.

NO MORE NATION-BUILDING

The GOP has unfortunately gained a reputation as "the war party." To many voters, the Republican Party has morphed into a party that is far too willing to throw American troops into any hot-spot around the world. The ultra-hawkishness of Lindsey Graham and John McCain and other Party leaders doesn't sit well with Americans who doubt that all this interventionism is sustainable or actually serves American interests.

Yes, the Republican Party is a patriotic party, and strongly supports our military, but it has also been, traditionally, a party that believes in the prudent use of force in defense of the national interest. It is the internationalist Democrats who have long been the Party of foreign interventionism, even as they weaken our defenses.

Trump is more of a foreign policy "realist" in that he believes that we should always put America's national interests first and that we should be wary of wars to promote democracy. Trump says, "We went from mistakes in Iraq to Egypt to Libya, to President Obama's line in the sand in Syria. Each of these actions...helped to throw the region into chaos, and gave ISIS the space it needs to grow and prosper."

Trump believes that in our effort to spread democracy in the Middle East and North Africa, "We tore up what institutions they had and then were surprised at what we unleashed. Civil war, religious fanaticism; thousands of American lives, and many trillions of dollars, were lost as a result. The vacuum was created that ISIS would fill. Iran, too, would rush in and fill the void, much to their unjust enrichment."

Many neocons responsible for the fiasco in Iraq are wailing about how Trump would be a disaster for American foreign policy, but of course *they* were the disaster for American foreign policy, discrediting the Republican Party, and helping to elect Barack Obama, and they have not shown much political wisdom since. Bill Kristol, publisher of the *Weekly Standard*, a leading neocon, and one of the most prominent voices for "never Trump," has been so wrong with his political predictions for so many years that the *Washington Post* dubbed him "a kind of cult figure of wrong." Robert Kagan, a foreign policy ally of Bill Kristol, has actually warned of a Trump dictatorship and crossed the aisle to endorse Hillary.[29] Men like Kagan and Kristol—and, if we're honest, about ninety percent of the pundits claiming to lead the conservative movement—should have their pundit licenses revoked for having been so wrong, so often, about so many issues and on so many predictions; for talking only amongst themselves (as if *they* are the conservative movement); and for denouncing Trump rather than trying to bring their self-proclaimed genius to help advise and guide him (they're too big for that). In private conversation, we've heard many neocons say that they'll back Hillary over Trump in November because at least she's not a know-nothing amateur. They should watch the movie *13 Hours* about Clinton's disaster in Benghazi to refresh their memory about what Hillary Clinton foreign policy looks like. If Trump is a know-nothing amateur, Hillary is a corrupt, mendacious, incompetent. We prefer the citizen-patriot Trump to a woman who cold-bloodedly sold American foreign policy for cash, as many writers have exposed.[30]

MAKE AMERICA SAFE AGAIN

During the Cold War, the U.S. government used an algebraic equation to measure how our country stood in comparison to others. Crafted by the CIA's Ray Cline, the mathematical formula held that: Perceived Power = [Population + Territory + Economy + Military] x [Strategy + Will].[31] Just consider how these factors have become devalued under President Obama's tenure:

- **Population and Territory:** Our population is growing, but largely through immigration, and we really have no idea how many immigrants are here illegally or for that matter how many actually share America's traditional culture and values. It's estimated that tens of thousands of illegal aliens cross our borders every month. Some are violent criminals; some are even Islamic terrorists from the Middle East. "In a report to Texas elected officials, the state Department of Public Safety says border security agencies have arrested Somali immigrants crossing the southern border who are known members of al-Shabab, the terrorist group that launched a deadly attack on the Westgate shopping mall in Nairobi, Kenya, and al-Itihaad al-Islamiya, another Somalia-based group once funded by Osama bin Laden," reports the *Washington Post*. "Another undocumented immigrant arrested crossing the border was on multiple U.S. terrorism watch lists."[32] Afghans and Pakistanis with terrorist ties who are on the FBI watch list have been apprehended at the border and, incomprehensibly, released by federal agents to disappear into our homeland.[33] Our population might be large, but it is certainly far less united by common bonds than it used to be, and our territorial integrity is violated every day by more than a thousand illegal immigrants.[34]

- **Economy:** We have about $20 trillion in debt (most of it held by Communist China),[35] annual federal budget deficits as high as $1.4 trillion, annual federal spending of nearly $4 trillion,[36] and almost 100 million Americans not in the workforce.[37] Our national debt is now higher than a whole year's gross domestic product, which is everything a country of 323 million buys, sells, builds, and consumes.[38] The economy is being systematically hollowed out.

- **Military:** It used to be American strategic doctrine that the United States maintained a military big enough to fight two wars in different parts of the globe at once. That's no longer the case.[39] America's military is overstretched and undermanned and the Obama administration seems more focused on putting women into combat than actually creating a large, well-equipped, combat-ready force. "The consistent decline in funding and the consequent shrinking of the force are putting it under significant pressure. Essential maintenance is being deferred; fewer units (mostly the Navy's platforms and the Special Operations Forces community) are being cycled through operational deployments more often and for longer periods; and old equipment is being extended while programmed replacements are problematic," reports the Heritage Foundation's *2015 Index of U.S. Military Strength*.[40] "The cumulative effect of such factors has resulted in a U.S. military that is marginally able to meet the demands of defending America's vital national interests."

- **Strategy:** Barack Obama has pushed a U.S. foreign policy based on his strategic principle of "leading from behind."[41] One doesn't have to be Henry Kissinger to figure out that leading from behind means not leading at all. And, in fact, as one newspaper put it, Obama's foreign policy, partly crafted by Hillary Clinton, might reasonably be dubbed "the worst foreign policy ever."[42]

- **Will:** Obama doesn't have it, or he wouldn't lead from behind and refuse to name our enemy in the war against Islamist terror. Hillary Clinton has the will to win the White House, but it is doubtful that someone so corrupt will earn much international respect or be seen as a reliable ally.

If Perceived Power = [Population + Territory + Economy + Military] x [Strategy + Will], then America is truly a power in decline.

We need a president who will make America great again, in part by making America safe again through a strong national defense. Trump has made clear that he intends to rebuild our military as Reagan did after years of neglect. It is no surprise to us that Trump is the favorite candidate of our active-duty military. According to a May 2016 poll of troops by the *Military Times*, Trump topped Hillary by a 2-to-1 margin.[43] That is no doubt because of his commitment to rebuild our armed forces but also because he will root out much of the political correctness that the Obama administration has imposed on the military. Trump will not waste American lives in pointless wars or "nation-building," but he will not be afraid to aggressively punish with swift military action America's sworn enemies who threaten our people with harm. No candidate is better placed to pursue a policy of peace through strength than Donald Trump. On defense issues, he is the closest thing we have to Ronald Reagan, who avoided unnecessary conflicts and built an American army and navy that was second to none, that deterred aggression, and that in the end brought us victory in the Cold War.

CHAPTER 9

Giving Back

The key to preserving Social Security is to have an economy that is robust and growing.

—Donald J. Trump

We will never be able to make America great again if we fail to make America solvent again. And this directly applies to the red ink spilling from entitlement programs. There is a way to do this without hurting the proverbial little guy—and Donald Trump has proposed it.

"We have to be very careful about changing the rules for those whose monthly checks make a big difference in their survival. A lot of people live from check to check. There's no way I'm letting those payments be reduced," Trump maintains. "This country made a deal with our citizens. That's their money.

129

They paid into the system their whole working lives so that older people could get their monthly checks."[1]

Trump has a responsible answer to ensure that the checks keeping coming.

FIX SOCIAL SECURITY

Trump's position is that our government is incredibly poorly managed. It should focus on its primary duties—national defense is one such; Social Security is now another—and trim the enormous layers of government fat that reside elsewhere. This is not to suggest that Social Security doesn't have serious problems that need to be rectified. Trump is well aware of this. He quipped almost twenty years ago, "More Americans under thirty believe in UFOs than believe in the long-term viability of Social Security. They know they are being lied to about this very important subject."[2]

Social Security has been badly run; it is facing tens of billions of dollars in shortfalls; but the Federal government also has an obligation to the American people who were told they could rely on it. "More than half of married couples and nearly three-quarters of unmarried Americans get more than 50 percent of their retirement income from the program," reports the *Motley Fool*. "More worrisome is that almost half of unmarried recipients rely on Social Security for more than 90 percent of their retirement income."[3] Without Social Security, 15 million seniors would immediately fall into poverty, according to the Center on Budget and Policy Priorities.

There are a lot of different proposals for how to tackle this disaster waiting to happen. Some want to dismantle Social Security and replace it completely with private accounts under control of the account holder. Others want to trim the benefits individuals receive or increase the age at which seniors can collect benefits.

Trump believes that cutting benefits, when people have been counting on them, is wrong. "We've got Social Security that's going to be destroyed if somebody like me doesn't bring money into the country," he says. "All these other people want to cut the hell out of it. I'm not going to cut it at all. I'm going to bring money in, and we're going to save it."[4]

He plans to save it by reviving America's economy and squeezing the waste, fraud, and abuse out of government entitlement programs.

The number one reform, he has said repeatedly, is turning our economy around, and putting the 100 million Americans (and potential taxpayers) who are out of work back on the job. As president, he sees a direct role for himself in this: "If we get tough and make the hard choices, we can make America a rich nation—and respected—once again. The right president can actually make America money by brokering big deals. We don't always think of our presidents as jobs and business negotiators, but they are. Presidents are our dealmakers in chief…The president's duty is to create an environment where free and fair markets can flourish, private sector jobs can be created, and our economy can boom. If they are strong negotiators and make the right deals, America wins,"[5] the tax-base increases, and the number of people on government relief falls.

Trump would also reform the tax code so that seniors aren't penalized for working or using investment income for retirement; give wealthy seniors the choice to opt out of Social Security they don't need; end the scam of illegal immigrants collecting government benefits; and make the biggest overhaul of government spending since Ronald Reagan launched the Grace Commission to root out government inefficiency.[6]

Donald Trump has always believed that private savings accounts are a better option than Social Security and that "privatization would be good for all of us," but he is also insistent that the American government not break faith with retirees.

REPEAL OBAMACARE

Trump has stated unequivocally that returning sanity to America's medical system begins with repealing Obamacare, which he sometimes calls the "UN-affordable" Care Act. "Obamacare is a catastrophe, and it has to be repealed and replaced. It was only approved because Obama lied 28 times saying you could keep your doctor and your plan."[7]

The Trump seven-point plan for reforming America's health care system includes not just repealing Obamacare, but replacing it with a much more consumer-focused, competitive system that would not force anyone to buy coverage they didn't want, that would allow insurance companies to compete across states, that would allow individual tax deductions for insurance premiums or have tax-free Health Savings Accounts, require price-transparency so that patients can compare the prices for health care (as we would with any other service or product), and other reforms.[8]

Trump sees Obamacare as a typical bureaucratic disaster. "There are now more than 100 codes for doctors to get reimbursement from insurance companies," he explains. One doctor told Trump, "I have more accountants and computer programmers working for me than I have nurses."

Trump says, "You want better plans at a better price? Increase competition for customers."[9] He will bring a businessman's mindset to putting America's health care system back in order.

SERVING VETERANS

After winning the war for American Independence, George Washington said, "The willingness with which our young people are likely to serve in any war, no matter how justified, shall be directly proportional to how they perceive veterans of earlier wars were treated and appreciated by our nation."

Donald Trump is a patriotic man, which is why reform of the ailing Veterans Administration was one of the first position papers released by his campaign. As he said, "The current state of the Department of Veterans Affairs is absolutely unacceptable."

In fact, it is a national disgrace. More than three hundred thousand veterans have died waiting for medical care from the Veterans Administration (VA).[10] "In one case, a veteran who applied for VA care in 1998 was placed in 'pending' status for 14 years," reports CNN. "Another veteran who passed away in 1988 was found to have an unprocessed record lingering in 2014." An investigation discovered that upwards of one million applications for veteran care were stalled, with many stuffed and forgotten in VA bureaucrats' desk drawers, with many Iraq and Afghanistan veterans losing eligibility for some care in the meantime.[11] Trump has made taking care of veterans a centerpiece of his run for the presidency. His campaign has raised and donated $5.6 million to veterans' charities (compared to Hillary Clinton, who gave a measly $70,000), and the outpouring of support he has received from former and serving military has been high.[12] Polls show him as far and away the favorite candidate of military personnel.

The Trump plan for helping veterans includes increasing veterans' programs for low-interest business loans and training to help veterans transition to the civilian workforce; massively reforming the current corrupt and outdated VA hospital system; ensuring that every VA hospital has an OBGYN ward so that women veterans don't get second class treatment; and setting up VA clinics in rural or underserved areas. The VA unfortunately has become a bureaucracy like any other, where bureaucrats, for instance, blew $6.3 million for fountains and statues at their offices while tales of VA scandals grew.[13]

Donald Trump will treat our nation's veterans as the heroes they are.

TRUMP'S HEART

Trump knows that "Our country is the greatest force for freedom the world has ever known," and that American freedom depends on courage, compassion, and intelligence.[14] Trump has made it clear that we have an honor-bound commitment to those who need medical care, and to our veterans. "Since our 'great' depression more than 80 years ago, America has always provided a social safety net for those who fall off the economic chart," Trump observes. "Retired seniors in particular rely on pensions and Social Security, as well as Medicare. We should not touch it. It's off the table."

But what is on the table is far more efficient management of programs that have been mismanaged for far too long, along with a far greater focus on actually helping seniors and veterans and those in need. Whether it is by the adoption of Medicare block grants to the states, which minimize bureaucracy and maximize benefits, or making veterans' issues a focal point of his administration, or rejuvenating America's economy so that we can afford programs like Social Security, Donald Trump is showing the true meaning of compassionate conservatism.

CHAPTER 10

Trump or a New Constitutional Convention

Many patriotic Americans feel that time is running short. They are desperate to save our country—and that's commendable.

Voting for Donald Trump is one very important way to restoring America's promise and improving its prospect for the future.

One enormous mistake some Americans seem tempted to make is to believe this election doesn't matter. Or for people to believe that electing Donald Trump president in 2016 is pointless and won't change anything. Some of these people, desperate and believing that the entire American government is broken, are advocating for a new constitution written by a new constitutional convention. This is a mistake.

We believe these desperate pleas are ignoring the good we can do immediately—and in desperation, Americans fruitlessly look for reform in all the wrong places.

We believe that a constitutional convention could turn out very badly for conservatives.

The goal of a new constitutional convention, or "Convention of States," as outlined and desired by some conservatives, would be to propose a series of amendments to "limit the authority and jurisdiction of the federal government." Since that was precisely the purpose of the U.S. Constitution we already have, there is no reason to surmise that some brand new language would do a better job than the most brilliant political thinkers in American history did at our nation's founding.

Article V of the Constitution has only twenty-two words about a convention for proposing amendments, but the most important is the word "call." Since only Congress can "call" the convention, it means that states have no control over who can be a delegate, who makes the rules, who sets the agenda, or who wields the gavel. Some conservatives assume that a constitutional convention would propose only conservative ideas like a balanced budget. It is just as likely, if not more so, that the Democrats would propose constitutional amendments to ensure socialized health care, or "free" higher education for everyone, or enshrining gay marriage into the Constitution—and how many Republicans would in the end capitulate so as not to seem "against" health care or education or "tolerance."

Less than a year before his untimely death, Supreme Court Justice Antonin Scalia called it a "horrible idea" to call a convention for proposing constitutional amendments. "Once you get those people together, you never know what they're going to do," the great justice warned. "You'll get everything but the kitchen sink written into the Constitution."

It's unrealistic to imagine some miraculous changes will occur through a constitutional process that voters cannot achieve at the ballot box. That's why conservative focus should be on winning the presidential election, not cracking open the Constitution for a round of editing.

The point is not to change the Constitution, the point is to enforce the Constitution on a wayward government, and to realize that if we are to achieve a renewed sense of national greatness, it is because we fight to defend and enshrine in our laws what is good and right. This battle hasn't been going our way lately. As Donald Trump has said, "The damage that Democrats, weak Republicans, and this disaster of a president

[Obama] have inflicted on America has put us in a mess like we've never seen before in our lifetimes."[1]

The mess the country is in has little to do with the Constitution, and a lot to do with the weakness of Republican politicians who seem never to see a fight they don't want to run from. Many of the economic arguments the country has had lately are arguments we thought we had already won in the Reagan era, only to see spendthrift Republicans destroy their reputation for economic competence. Much of the social revolution we've endured has actually been put into law by judges appointed by Republicans. And the Republican Congress might as well have been a Democratic Congress for all it has done to rein in Obama's budget demands and executive orders.

America has been—and is being—profoundly changed without the support of the people.

That is why we need a conservative "revolution." Yes, we know how ironic it can sound for "conservatives" to be calling for a "revolution." But in America, certainly, the two words can go together. The American Revolution was an uprising to conserve and restore the colonists' "rights of Englishmen." The Reagan Revolution was a movement to conserve and restore the principles that had made America great. The Trump Revolution follows in that pattern—it is a *conservative* revolt to conserve and restore American greatness.

The Trump Revolution is about building America back up rather than tearing her down as a place that needs to be fundamentally transformed as Obama pledged to do. The Trump Revolution is about ending the lies of political correctness, so that we can deal honestly with the serious problems we face. And the Trump Revolution is about finally giving voice—and providing action—for the majority of American people who have been ignored by a political establishment more interested in serving itself and its own aims rather than the needs, wants, and desires of the voters.

In the end, it is really about affirming American Exceptionalism—reminding ourselves, and acting on the principle, that America is a force for good and a place that has rewarded many, rather than the horribly guilty, racist, sexist country of leftist mythology.

"America and dreams—hopes, aspirations, ambitions—have been tied together from the beginning," writes Dr. James S. Robbins in his book on American exceptionalism, *Native Americans*. "In the classic vision, America is a land of economic opportunity, a place where individuals could prosper and each generation would be able to live better than the one that came before." This belief is what we need to restore, and we believe that Trump will be a conservative, energetic restorer of the American Dream.

It is this we need, not a "convention of states."

"Freedom is a fragile thing and is never more than one generation away from extinction," then-Governor Ronald Reagan warned. "It is not ours by inheritance; it must be fought for and defended constantly by each generation, for it comes only once to a people. Those who have known freedom and then lost it have never known it again."[2]

The sense of urgency that Reagan conveyed a half century ago is felt by Donald Trump. He knows that if liberty's defenders don't step forward now, if we do not win in 2016, America as we know it could be finished; and at most we will be left with cinematic fragments of what once was, watching old Hollywood films...starring Ronald Reagan.

The 2016 election is not just a contest between two political parties but a showdown between two visions for our America. Senator Jeff Sessions believes, "This election will be the last chance for Americans to get control of their government." Donald Trump's vision is distinct and puts America First and subordinates government to the people. It is time to take back our country. The Revolution starts not in a dreamed-of convention of states, but now, in November, at the ballot box, with a vote for Trump.

Conclusion

I see huge challenges before us. But I also see a nation that has survived everything fate has thrown at it and come out better every time.

—Donald J. Trump

"We are at a critical turning point in our history, not only for you and me but for our children as well. America may be struggling, it may be crippled, but we can rise again. Our time has not passed, it is here, and the potential is amazing."[1] Donald Trump is a realist, but also an optimist. "America's best days are still to come," he promises. But only if we make the tough decisions we have to make now.

When he was considering a run for the presidency in 2000, Trump wrote that, "The Republicans and Democrats have demonstrated they lack the courage and the will to help you. If you want something done about this, you have to find someone else to support— someone who is not tied to, or terrified by, the interest groups supporting the status quo."[2]

Conservatives know that feeling very well. We elected a Republican Congress—first a House and then a Senate—and Congress did essentially nothing to stop Obama's revolutionary efforts to fundamentally transform America. The House did not use the power of the purse to stop Obama and the Senate seemed feckless in opposition to Obama's executive over-reach. When the Supreme Court re-wrote laws, Congress wrung its hands but refused to use its Article I power to defund, limit jurisdiction or even impeach. These so-called conservative leaders failed to lead.

We find it deeply ironic now that so many of these failed "conservative" politicians in Congress and on the national scene are so critical of Donald Trump especially because Trump is now best known for what they are lacking: 1) getting things done, and 2) thinking and acting outside of politically correct parameters.

Let's be clear: for too long, both parties have failed to balance the budget, secure our borders, and failed to enact policies that liberate entrepreneurs to create businesses and jobs. The Republican Party, meanwhile, has failed to put any breaks on the Democrats' social radicalism, so that even our military has become a hothouse of political correctness; and in the course of Obama's eight years in office, we have had the meaning of marriage overturned, we have had the federal government demand unisex access to restrooms, changing rooms, and locker rooms in our public schools, and we have had the religious freedom of orthodox Christians and Jews put under threat, with their beliefs on marriage and sex treated as bigotry in law and in our public schools.

"This is a binary choice," says John R. Bolton, the former permanent U.S. representative to the United Nations, and a widely respected conservative. "The next president will either be Donald Trump or Hillary Clinton, unless Hillary gets indicted. Talk about a third-party candidate is badly misplaced. The idea of not voting at all is no better because, functionally, that's a vote for Hillary."[3]

Phil Jennings, an investment banker, novelist, and a former Marine Corps pilot in Vietnam who also flew missions for the CIA-sponsored Air America in Laos, wrote a piece for Breitbart.com in which he said "when I hear Republican and conservative elites lecture the rest of us about Trump's supposed deviations from their ideological strictures, or his shortcomings as a human being, I think about what Jesus said about casting the first stone. I seriously doubt any of these critics would be able to stand up to the same type of scrutiny they are giving Trump, assuming they had the guts to get into the arena..."

After laying out how Trump's flaws are inconsequential compared to Hillary's lying, deceit, corruption, and ideological leftism, Jennings concludes: "I don't pretend to know if God would vote for Donald Trump, or for that matter what state He is registered to vote in. But I do know that the God of Abraham who shed his grace on America had a purpose and a vision. He would not turn his back on a country and a people that has achieved so much under his blessings. Donald Trump wants to make America great again, and so far as I know, if he did he would be doing God's work."[4]

That's something to which every conservative should be able to say: Amen.

Acknowledgments

The authors would like to thank Donald J. Trump for the time he has given us to discuss his ideas for how to make America great again.

At Regnery, we would like to express our gratitude to Vice President and Executive Editor Harry Crocker, whose sympathetic ear, even more sympathetic editing, and commitment to the book were essential to getting the job done on a tight deadline. Our thanks also go out to President Marji Ross, Senior Managing Editor Maria Ruhl, and Copy Editor Joseph Francis for their support for this project.

We are eternally thankful for the Founders' vision for a country based on the right to life, liberty, and the pursuit of happiness. We have a republic if we can keep it.

PHYLLIS SCHLAFLY: To the many people who contributed to the victories that I and Eagle Forum have had over the years. Together, we helped to create the conservative movement in 1964 with *A Choice Not an Echo* and we have built a unique conservative organization of volunteers who are motivated to do their part to make America great again. Finally, thank you to Senator Jeff Sessions for putting Americans first. History will honor his leadership and love of our nation.

ED MARTIN: Thank you to my wife Carol for her love and support; and to our four children for their patience and joy. I owe special thanks to my parents, Ed and Virginia Martin, and my in-laws Mike and Mary Alice Reyburn. To work for Phyllis Schlafly is a highlight of my life and I thank her and all my colleagues in the Eagle Forum family.

BRETT M. DECKER: Having an archipelago of guest rooms in beautiful and faraway locales, where one can hide from the world, is essential for writing a book. For providing food, drink, shelter, and seclusion, I am beholden to: Denise and Louis Joseph in Palm Beach, Florida; Brian Nova of P.O. Camp; Dr.

Eric Mizrahi in Marina del Rey, California; and Mary
Sult and Anthony Welcher in Palm Desert, California.

Special shout-outs are telegraphed to: Richard Dia-
mond for his all-consuming preoccupation with petty
tyranny; Amy and Ken Wolfe for letting me borrow a
precious volume from their collection; Robert Powers
for hunting down a couple old quotes; Madison Miller
for digging up some articles; Rev. Mr. James M.
Smith, FSSP, for his prayers from Our Lady of Gua-
dalupe Seminary; Tina Dupuy for simply being Tina
Dupuy; Newsmax founder Chris Ruddy for his gen-
erosity of spirit and pragmatic perspective; Van Hipp
for putting himself out there; Robert F. Agostinelli for
his friendship and forthrightness; and Dr. James S.
Robbins for late-night bull sessions and for checking
in on Chop Suey and Van Winkle the Cat when I'm
away.

For all of their support in everything, I send love
back to my family: Sharon Rose Decker, the late John
Erie Decker, Sandra Decker, Jarett Decker, Steve
Decker, Ronald Forsberg, and Dina, Sasha, Nick,
Chelsea, and Chris.

For Missey Condie, whose knowledge, inquisitive-
ness, and belief in the superiority of America are
inspiring.

Trump 5 Questions With Brett M. Decker

Lack of leadership is the biggest threat to America.
Washington Times: Monday, October 15, 2012

Donald Trump is one of the world's most recognized business leaders. With a reputation built on real-estate development, his luxury towers dominate big-city skylines, and his hotels and golf courses are prime destinations for the well-heeled. In recent years, Mr. Trump has become a broadcast powerhouse on NBC with his hit television show *The Apprentice* and major beauty pageants such as Miss USA and Miss Universe. An articulate voice in national politics, anticipation over a Trump presidential bid shook up the 2012 Republican primary contest. Author of numerous bestsellers including 1987's iconic *The Art of the Deal*, Mr. Trump's newest book is, *Time to Get Tough: Making America #1 Again* (Regnery, 2011). You can find out more about the Trump empire at trump.com and donaldjtrump.com.

Decker: You are one of the rare prominent voices out there insisting that rebuilding our manufacturing base is central to renewing America as an economic power. As a Detroiter, this really jumps out at me, but manufacturing is not something one hears Republicans talking about very often. What do you think needs to be done on this front?

Trump: The outsourcing of jobs has greatly diminished our power and has to be addressed. Our dealings with China have been ridiculous as I've made clear. Our core as a country was built around industries that were built here and that thrived here. That has eroded to such a degree that our structure has crumbled and needs to be reinforced. As a builder, I would compare it to a building that has been left unattended, or neglected, and therefore requires more attention to repair. We need entrepreneurs to keep— or to return—our economic power to where it should be. As Henry Ford said, "Don't find fault, find a remedy." The remedy is a strong manufacturing base, which means more jobs. It's not complicated.

Decker: You're refreshingly tough on the People's Republic. In your book, you write, "Get it straight:

China is not our friend." Why is Beijing a menace to the United States, and how should we counter this communist state?

Trump: They've taken every opportunity possible to rip us off, and they've been given that opportunity by Obama and his administration. Sometimes it appears Obama officials are clueless, but one thing for sure is that they are bad negotiators. China's manipulation of currency has been consistent with obvious results to be seen in our steel industry, as one example, and they steal our technology. The list goes on—they have no scruples when it comes to business and are aggressive in their striving for power. What we need is a strong leader who knows how to negotiate, and who understands how business works and how businesses are built. We also need a leader who understands the threat that China poses. It's hard to believe the current administration is fully aware of the situation.

Decker: Chapter 7 of your book is titled, "A Safety Net, Not a Hammock." The U.S. national debt has surpassed $16 trillion because too many people expect government to give them goodies. Do you worry that Americans have gotten too lazy, complacent or just lost the character it will take to turn this mess around?

Trump: I don't think Americans have gotten lazy, as many people are looking for work. It's hard to go to work if there aren't any jobs. Outsourcing has hurt us tremendously. The unmitigated greed of certain individuals such as [convicted multi-billion-dollar fraudster Bernie] Madoff and the rampant Wall Street shenanigans have damaged many people and made people untrusting and wary, and rightly so. But I also believe that self-reliance needs to be emphasized and everyone needs to be vigilant. America has been blessed in very many ways and that can't be taken for granted. I know America can be great again, but it will require focus and hard work.

Decker: As the son of a Ford Motor Company executive, I grew up believing that the business of America is business. It now increasingly seems that government is the senior partner in the public-private-sector relationship. How is today's out of control bureaucracy a drag on U.S. competitiveness and the entrepreneurial spirit that made this country great?

Trump: As you mention, the entrepreneurial spirit made this country great. We grew by leaps and bounds when that spirit was encouraged. Now look at it! I built my own empire. No one else built it for me. I've provided tens of thousands of jobs. I was and remain competitive because that is what is required. I know people are grateful to have jobs and my job is to provide those jobs. I think most people would rather work than get a handout or remain idle. Bureaucracy has slowed things down considerably, and as someone who is used to getting things done, and quickly, it's very apparent that the government has not been helpful. They have not been encouraging to the new generation. Some of Obama's comments have made it sound as if building something is undesirable. Our young people need to know what made this country great to begin with: entrepreneurs. My father, Fred C. Trump, had a four-step formula for success that works: Get in, Get it done, Get it done right, and Get out. That keeps the momentum going, and one thing this country needs is more momentum.

Decker: What do you think is the most imminent threat facing America today, and what should be done to address the problem?

Trump: Lack of leadership is the biggest threat. That covers a lot of territory. In order for a country to thrive, there can't be weakness at the top. Other countries know we have a weak leader and it's easy to become a target in those circumstances, China being a good example. Our military forces have to remain intact and effective and have the right leadership. Our business leaders need to be encouraged. Obama has not addressed our problems in a way that has produced results. He has not provided us with solutions— just more problems. He is responsible for a decline in this country that has been unprecedented. The way to address this problem is to have a strong leader who knows what is going on and has the intelligence and strength to deal with it.

Donald J. Trump Addresses Terrorism, Immigration, and National Security

June 13, 2016, Manchester, New Hampshire

Thank you for joining me today.

This was going to be a speech on Hillary Clinton and how bad a President, especially in these times of Radical Islamic Terrorism, she would be.

Even her former Secret Service Agent, who has seen her under pressure and in times of stress, has stated that she lacks the temperament and integrity to be president.

There will be plenty of opportunity to discuss these important issues at a later time, and I will deliver that speech soon.

But today there is only one thing to discuss: the growing threat of terrorism inside of our borders.

The attack on the Pulse Nightclub in Orlando, Florida, was the worst terrorist strike on our soil since September 11th, and the worst mass shooting in our country's history.

So many people dead, so many people gravely injured, so much carnage, such a disgrace.

The horror is beyond description.

The families of these wonderful people are totally devastated. Likewise, our whole nation, and indeed the whole world, is devastated.

We express our deepest sympathies to the victims, the wounded, and their families.

We mourn, as one people, for our nation's loss— and pledge our support to any and all who need it.

I would like to ask now that we all observe a moment of silence for the victims of the attack.

[SILENCE]

Our nation stands together in solidarity with the members of Orlando's LGBT Community.

This is a very dark moment in America's history.

A radical Islamic terrorist targeted the nightclub not only because he wanted to kill Americans, but in order to execute gay and lesbian citizens because of their sexual orientation.

It is a strike at the heart and soul of who we are as a nation.

It is an assault on the ability of free people to live their lives, love who they want and express their identity.

It is an attack on the right of every single American to live in peace and safety in their own country.

We need to respond to this attack on America as one united people—with force, purpose and determination.

But the current politically correct response cripples our ability to talk and think and act clearly.

<u>If we don't get tough, and we don't get smart—and fast—we're not going to have a country anymore—there will be nothing left.</u>

The killer, whose name I will not use, or ever say, was born to Afghan parents who immigrated to the United States. His father published support for the Afghan Taliban, a regime which murders those who don't share its radical views. The father even said he was running for President of that country.

The bottom line is that the only reason the killer was in America in the first place was because we allowed his family to come here.

That is a fact, and it's a fact we need to talk about.

We have a dysfunctional immigration system which does not permit us to know who we let into our country, and it does not permit us to protect our citizens.

We have an incompetent administration, and if I am not elected President, that will not change over the next four years—but it must change, and it must change now.

With fifty people dead, and dozens more wounded, we cannot afford to talk around the issue anymore—we have to address it head on.

I called for a ban after San Bernardino, and was met with great scorn and anger but now, many are saying I was right to do so—and although the pause is temporary, we must find out what is going on. The ban will be lifted when we as a nation are in a position to properly and perfectly screen those people coming into our country.

The immigration laws of the United States give the President the power to suspend entry into the country of any class of persons that the President deems detrimental to the interests or security of the United States, as he deems appropriate.

I will use this power to protect the American people. When I am elected, I will suspend immigration from areas of the world when there is a proven history of terrorism against the United States, Europe or our allies, until we understand how to end these threats.

After a full, impartial and long overdue security assessment, we will develop a responsible immigration policy that serves the interests and values of America.

We cannot continue to allow thousands upon thousands of people to pour into our country, many of whom have the same thought process as this savage killer.

Many of the principles of Radical Islam are incompatible with Western values and institutions.

Radical Islam is anti-woman, anti-gay and anti-American.

I refuse to allow America to become a place where gay people, Christian people, and Jewish people, are the targets of persecution and intimidation by Radical Islamic preachers of hate and violence.

It's not just a national security issue. It is a quality of life issue.

If we want to protect the quality of life for all Americans—women and children, gay and straight, Jews and Christians and all people—then we need to tell the truth about Radical Islam.

We need to tell the truth, also, about how Radical Islam is coming to our shores.

We are importing Radical Islamic Terrorism into the West through a failed immigration system—and through an intelligence community held back by our president.

Even our own FBI Director has admitted that we cannot effectively check the backgrounds of the people we are letting into America.

All of the September 11th hijackers were issued visas.

Large numbers of Somali refugees in Minnesota have tried to join ISIS.

The Boston Bombers came here through political asylum.

The male shooter in San Bernardino—again, whose name I won't mention—was the child of immigrants from Pakistan, and he brought his wife—the other terrorist—from Saudi Arabia, through another one of our easily exploited visa programs.

Immigration from Afghanistan into the United States has increased nearly five-fold in just one year. According to Pew Research, 99% of people in Afghanistan support oppressive Sharia Law.

We admit many more from other countries in the region who share these same oppressive views.

If we want to remain a free and open society, then we have to control our borders.

Yet, Hillary Clinton—for months and despite so many attacks—repeatedly refused to even say the words "Radical Islam," until I challenged her yesterday to say the words or leave the race.

However, Hillary Clinton—who has been forced to say the words today after policies she supports have caused us so much damage—still has no clue what

Radical Islam is, and won't speak honestly about what it is.

She is in total denial, and her continuing reluctance to ever name the enemy broadcasts weakness across the world.

In fact, just a few weeks before the San Bernardino slaughter, Hillary Clinton explained her refusal to say the words Radical Islam. Here is what she said: "Muslims are peaceful and tolerant people, and have nothing whatsoever to do with terrorism."

Hillary Clinton says the solution is to ban guns. They tried that in France, which has among the toughest gun laws in the world, and 130 were brutally murdered by Islamic terrorists in cold blood. Her plan is to disarm law-abiding Americans, abolishing the 2nd Amendment, and leaving only the bad guys and terrorists with guns. She wants to take away Americans' guns, then admit the very people who want to slaughter us.

I will be meeting with the NRA, which has given me their earliest endorsement in a Presidential race, to discuss how to ensure Americans have the means to protect themselves in this age of terror.

The bottom line is that Hillary supports the policies that bring the threat of Radical Islam into America, and allow it to grow overseas.

Even a single individual can be devastating, just look at what happened in Orlando. Can you imagine large groups?

Truly, our President doesn't know what he is doing. He has failed us, and failed us badly, and under his leadership, this situation will not get any better—it will only get worse.

Each year, the United States permanently admits more than 100,000 immigrants from the Middle East, and many more from Muslim countries outside the Middle East. Our government has been admitting ever-growing numbers, year after year, without any effective plan for our security.

In fact, Clinton's State Department was in charge of the admissions process for people applying to enter from overseas.

Having learned nothing from these attacks, she now plans to massively increase admissions without a screening plan, including a 500% increase in Syrian refugees.

This could be a better, bigger version of the legendary Trojan Horse.

We can't let this happen.

Altogether, under the Clinton plan, you'd be admitting hundreds of thousands of refugees from the Middle East with no system to vet them, or to prevent the radicalization of their children.

The burden is on Hillary Clinton to tell us why she believes immigration from these dangerous countries should be increased without any effective system to screen who we are bringing in.

The burden is on Hillary Clinton to tell us why we should admit anyone into our country who supports violence of any kind against gay and lesbian Americans.

The burden is also on Hillary Clinton to tell us how she will pay for it. Her plan will cost Americans hundreds of billions of dollars long-term.

Wouldn't this money be better spent on rebuilding America for our current population, including the many poor people already living here?

We have to stop the tremendous flow of Syrian refugees into the United States—we don't know who they are, they have no documentation, and we don't know what they're planning.

What I want is common sense. I want a mainstream immigration policy that promotes American values.

That is the choice I put before the American people: a mainstream immigration policy designed to benefit America, or Hillary Clinton's radical immigration policy designed to benefit politically-correct special interests.

We've got to get smart, and tough, and vigilant, and we've got to do it now, because <u>later is too late</u>.

Ask yourself, who is really the friend of women and the LGBT community, Donald Trump with his actions, or Hillary Clinton with her words? Clinton wants to allow Radical Islamic terrorists to pour into our country—they enslave women, and murder gays.

<u>I don't want them in our country.</u>

The terrorist attack on the Pulse Night Club demands a full and complete investigation into every aspect of the assault.

In San Bernardino, as an example, people knew what was going on, but they used the excuse of racial profiling for not reporting it.

We need to know what the killer discussed with his relatives, parents, friends and associates.

We need to know if he was affiliated with any radical Mosques or radical activists and what, if any, is their immigration status.

We need to know if he travelled anywhere, and who he travelled with.

We need to make sure every single last person involved in this plan—including anyone who knew something but didn't tell us—is brought to justice.

If it can be proven that somebody had information about any attack, and did not give this information to authorities, they must serve prison time.

America must do more—much more—to protect its citizens, especially people who are potential victims of crimes based on their backgrounds or sexual orientations.

It also means we must change our foreign policy.

The decision to overthrow the regime in Libya, then pushing for the overthrow of the regime in Syria, among other things, without plans for the day after, have created space for ISIS to expand and grow.

These actions, along with our disastrous Iran deal, have also reduced our ability to work in partnership with our Muslim allies in the region.

That is why our new goal must be to defeat Islamic terrorism, not nation-building.

For instance, the last major NATO mission was Hillary Clinton's war in Libya. That mission helped unleash ISIS on a new continent.

I've said NATO needs to change its focus to stopping terrorism. Since I've raised that criticism, NATO has since announced a new initiative focused on just that.

America must unite the whole civilized world in the fight against Islamic terrorism, just like we did against communism in the Cold War.

We've tried it President Obama's way. <u>He gave the world his apology tour, we got ISIS, and many other problems, in return.</u>

I'd like to conclude my remarks today by again expressing our solidarity with the people of Orlando who have come under attack.

When I am President, I pledge to protect and defend all Americans who live inside of our borders. Wherever they come from, wherever they were born, all Americans living here and following our laws will be protected.

America will be a tolerant and open society.

America will also be a safe society.

We will protect our borders at home.

We will defeat ISIS overseas.

We will ensure every parent can raise their children in peace and safety.

We will make America rich again.

We will make America safe again.

We will make American Great Again.

Thank you.

The media talks about "homegrown," terrorism, but Islamic radicalism, and the networks that nurture it, are imports from overseas.

Yes, there are many radicalized people already inside our country as a result of the poor policies of the past. But the whole point is that it will be much, much easier to deal with our current problem if we don't keep on bringing in people who add to the problem.

For instance, the controversial Mosque attended by the Boston Bombers had as its founder an immigrant from overseas charged in an assassination plot.

This shooter in Orlando was the child of an immigrant father who supported one of the most repressive regimes on Earth. Why would we admit people who support violent hatred?

Hillary Clinton can never claim to be a friend of the gay community as long as she continues to support immigration policies that bring Islamic extremists to our country who suppress women, gays and anyone who doesn't share their views.

She can't have it both ways. She can't claim to be supportive of these communities while trying to increase the number of people coming in who want to oppress them.

How does this kind of immigration make our life better?

How does this kind of immigration make our country better?

Why does Hillary Clinton want to bring people here—in vast numbers—who reject our values?

Immigration is a privilege, and we should not let anyone into this country who doesn't support our communities—all of our communities.

America has already admitted four times more immigrants than any country on earth, and we continue to admit millions more with no real checks or scrutiny.

Not surprisingly, wages for our workers haven't budged in many years.

So whether it's matter of national security, or financial security, we can't afford to keep on going like this. We owe $19 trillion in debt, and no longer have options.

All our communities, from all backgrounds, are ready for some relief. This is not an act of offense against anyone; it is an act of defense.

I want us all to work together, including in partnership with our Muslim communities. But Muslim communities must cooperate with law enforcement and turn in the people who they know are bad—and they do know where they are.

I want to fix our schools, roads, bridges and job market. I want every American to succeed. Hillary Clinton wants to empty out the Treasury to bring people into the country that include individuals who preach hate against our own citizens.

I want to protect our citizens—all of our citizens.

Donald J. Trump: An America First Energy Plan

May 26, 2016, Bismarck, North Dakota

I'm delighted to be in North Dakota, a state at the forefront of a new energy revolution.

Oil and natural gas production is up significantly in the last decade. Our oil imports have been cut in half.

But all this occurred in spite of massive new bureaucratic and political barriers.

President Obama has done everything he can to get in the way of American energy. He's made life much more difficult for North Dakota, as costly regulation makes it harder and harder to turn a profit.

If Hillary Clinton is in charge, things will get much worse. She will shut down energy production across this country.

Millions of jobs, and trillions of dollars of wealth, will be destroyed as a result. That is why our choice this November is so crucial.

Here's what it comes down to.

Wealth versus poverty.

North Dakota shows how energy exploration creates shared prosperity. Better schools. More funding for infrastructure. Higher wages. Lower unemployment.

Things we've been missing.

It's a choice between sharing in this great energy wealth, or sharing in the poverty promised by Hillary Clinton.

You don't have to take my word for it. Just listen to Hillary Clinton's own words. She has declared war on the American worker.

Here is what Hillary Clinton said earlier this year: "We are going to put a lot of coal miners and coal companies out of work."

She wants to shut down the coal mines.

And if Crooked Hillary can shut down the mines, she can shut down your business too.

Let me tell you how President Obama Undermined Our Middle Class

President Obama's stated intent is to eliminate oil and natural gas production in America.

His policy is death by a thousand cuts through an onslaught of regulations.

The Environmental Protection Agency's use of totalitarian tactics forces energy operators in North Dakota into paying unprecedented multi-billion dollar fines before a penalty is even confirmed.

Government misconduct goes on and on:

- The Department of Justice filed a lawsuit against seven North Dakota oil companies for the deaths of 28 birds while the Administration fast-tracked wind projects that kill more than 1 million birds a year.
- The U.S Fish and Wildlife Service abuses the Endangered Species Act to restrict oil and gas exploration.
- Adding to the pain, President Obama now proposes a $10-per-barrel tax on American-produced oil in the middle of a downturn.

At the same time President Obama lifts economic sanctions on Iran, he imposes economic sanctions on America. He has allowed this country to hit the lowest oil rig count since 1999, producing thousands of lay-offs.

America's incredible energy potential remains untapped. It is a totally self-inflicted wound.

Under my presidency, we will accomplish complete American energy independence.

Imagine a world in which our foes, and the oil cartels, can no longer use energy as a weapon.

But President Obama has done everything he can to keep us dependent on others. Let me list some of the good energy projects he killed.

He rejected the Keystone XL Pipeline despite the fact that:

- It would create and support more than 42,000 jobs.
- His own State Department concluded that it would be the safest pipeline ever built in the United States.
- And it would have no significant impact on the environment.
- Yet, even as he rejected this America-Canada pipeline, he made a deal that allows Iran to transport more oil through its pipeline that would have ever flowed through Keystone—with no environmental review.

President Obama has done everything he can to kill the coal industry. Here are a few of President Obama's decrees:

Regulations that shut down hundreds of coal-fired power plants and block the construction of new ones.

A prohibition against coal production on federal land.

Draconian climate rules that, unless stopped, would effectively bypass Congress to impose job-killing cap-and-trade.

President Obama has aggressively blocked the production of oil and natural gas:

- He's taken a huge percentage of the Alaska National Petroleum Reserve off the table.
- Oil and natural gas production on federal lands is down 10%.
- 87% of available land in the Outer Continental Shelf has been put off limits.
- Atlantic Lease sales were closed down too—despite the fact that they would create 280,000 jobs and $23.5 billion in economic activity.
- President Obama entered the United States into the Paris Climate Accords—

unilaterally, and without the permission
of Congress. This agreement gives foreign bureaucrats control over how much
energy we use right here in America.

These actions have denied millions of Americans
access to the energy wealth sitting under our feet. This
is your treasure, and you—the American People—are
entitled to share in the riches. President Obama's anti-
energy orders have also weakened our security, by
keeping us reliant on foreign sources of energy. Every
dollar of energy we don't explore here, is a dollar of
energy that makes someone else rich over there. If
President Obama wanted to weaken America he
couldn't have done a better job.

***As bad as President Obama is, Hillary Clinton
will be worse.***

- She will escalate the war against American energy, and unleash the EPA to
  control every aspect of our lives.
- She declared that "we've got to move
  away from coal and all the other fossil
  fuels," locking away trillions in American wealth.
- In March, Hillary Clinton said: "by the
  time we get through all of my conditions,

I do not think there will be many places in America where fracking will continue to take place." Keep in mind, shale energy production could add 2 million jobs in 7 years.

Yet, while Hillary Clinton doesn't want American energy, she is strongly in favor of foreign energy. Here is what she told China as Secretary of State:

- "American experts and Chinese experts will work to develop China's natural gas resources. Imagine what it would mean for China if China unleashed its own natural gas resources so you are not dependent on foreign oil."

Hillary Clinton has her priorities wrong. But we are going to turn all of that around.

A Trump Administration will develop an America First energy plan. Here is how this plan will make America Wealthy Again:

- <u>American energy dominance will be declared a strategic economic and foreign policy goal of the United States</u>.

- America has 1.5 times as much oil as the combined proven resources of all OPEC countries; we have more Natural Gas than Russia, Iran, Qatar and Saudi Arabia Combined; we have three times more coal than Russia. Our total untapped oil and gas reserves on federal lands equal an estimated $50 trillion.

- <u>We will become, and stay, totally independent of any need to import energy from the OPEC cartel or any nations hostile to our interests</u>.

- At the same time, we will work with our Gulf allies to develop a positive energy relationship as part of our anti-terrorism strategy.

- <u>We will use the revenues from energy production to rebuild our roads, schools, bridges and public infrastructure</u>. Cheaper energy will also boost American agriculture.

- <u>We will get the bureaucracy out of the way of innovation, so we can pursue all forms of energy</u>. This includes renewable energies and the technologies of the future. It includes nuclear, wind and solar energy—but not to the exclusion of other energy. The government should not pick winners and losers. Instead, it should remove obstacles to exploration. Any market has ups and downs, but lifting these draconian barriers will ensure that we are no longer at the mercy of global markets.

A Trump Administration will focus on real environmental challenges, not phony ones:

- We will reject Hillary Clinton's poverty-expansion agenda that enriches her friends and makes everyone else poor.
- We'll solve *real* environmental problems in our communities like the need for clean and safe drinking water. President Obama actually tried to cut the funding for our drinking water infrastructure—even as he pushed to increase funding for his EPA bureaucrats.
- American workers will be the ones building this new infrastructure.

Here is my 100-day action plan:

- We're going to rescind all the job-destroying Obama executive actions including the Climate Action Plan and the Waters of the U.S. rule.
- We're going to save the coal industry and other industries threatened by Hillary Clinton's extremist agenda.
- I'm going to ask Trans Canada to renew its permit application for the Keystone Pipeline.
- We're going to lift moratoriums on energy production in federal areas.
- We're going to revoke policies that impose unwarranted restrictions on new drilling technologies. These technologies create millions of jobs with a smaller footprint than ever before.
- We're going to cancel the Paris Climate Agreement and stop all payments of U.S. tax dollars to U.N. global warming programs.
- Any regulation that is outdated, unnecessary, bad for workers, or contrary to the national interest, <u>will be scrapped</u>. We will also eliminate duplication, provide regulatory certainty, and trust local officials and local residents.

- Any future regulation will go through a simple test: is this regulation good for the American worker? If it doesn't pass this test, the rule will not be approved.

Policy decisions will be public and transparent. They won't be made on Hillary's private email account.

We're going to do all this while taking proper regard for rational environmental concerns. We are going to conserve our beautiful natural habitats, reserves and resources.

In a Trump Administration, political activists with extreme agendas will no longer write the rules. Instead, we will work with conservationists whose only agenda is protecting nature.

From an environmental standpoint, my priorities are very simple: clean air and clean water.

My America First energy plan will do for the American People what Hillary Clinton will never do: create real jobs and real wage growth.

According to the Institute for Energy Research, lifting the restrictions on American energy will create a flood of new jobs:

- Almost a $700 billion increase in annual economic output over the next 30 years.

- More than a $30 billion increase in annual wages over the next 7 years.
- Over the next four decades, more than $20 trillion in additional economic activity and $6 trillion in new tax revenue.

The oil and natural gas industry supports 10 million high-paying Americans jobs and can create another 400,000 new jobs per year. This exploration will also create a resurgence in American manufacturing—dramatically reducing both our trade deficit and our budget deficit. Compare this future to Hillary Clinton's Venezuela-style politics of poverty.

If you think about it, not one idea Hillary Clinton has will actually create a single net job or create a single new dollar to put in workers' pockets.

In fact, every idea Hillary has will make jobs disappear.

Hillary Clinton's agenda is job destruction. My agenda is job creation.

She wants to tax and regulate our workers to the point of extinction.

She wants terrible trade deals, like NAFTA, signed by her husband, that will empty out our manufacturing.

During her time as Secretary of State, she surrendered to China—allowing them to steal hundreds of billions of dollars in our intellectual property.

She let them devalue their currency and add more than a trillion dollars to our trade deficit.

Then there was Libya.

Secretary Clinton's reckless Libya invasion handed the country over to ISIS, which now controls the oil.

The Middle East that Clinton inherited was far less dangerous than the Middle East she left us with today.

Her reckless decisions in Iraq, Libya, Iran, Egypt and Syria have made the Middle East more unstable than ever before.

The Hillary Clinton foreign policy legacy is chaos.

Hillary Clinton also wants totally open borders in America, which would further plunge our workers into poverty.

Hillary's open borders agenda means a young single mom living in poverty would have to compete for a job or a raise against millions of lower-wage workers rushing into the country, but she doesn't care.

My agenda will be accomplished through a series of reforms that put America First:

- Energy reform that creates trillions in new wealth.

- Immigration reform that protects our borders and defends our workers.
- Tax reform that brings millions of new jobs to America.
- Regulation reform that eliminates stupid rules that send our jobs overseas.
- Welfare reform that requires employers to recruit from the unemployment office—not the immigration office.
- Trade reform that brings back our manufacturing jobs and stands up to countries that cheat.

There is one more thing we must do to make America wealthy again: we have to make our communities safe again.

Violent crime is rising in major cities across the country. This is unacceptable. Every parent has the right to raise their kids in safety.

When we put political correctness before justice, we hurt those who have the least. It undermines their schools, slashes the value of their homes, and drives away their jobs.

Crime is a stealth tax on the poor.

To those living in fear, I say: help is coming. A Trump Administration will return law and order to

America. Security is not something that should only be enjoyed by the rich and powerful.

By the way, I was endorsed by the National Rifle Association, and we are not going to let Hillary Clinton abolish the 2nd Amendment, either.

My reform agenda is going to bring wealth and security to the poorest communities in this country.

What does Hillary have to offer the poor but more of the same?

In Chicago, for instance, one-fourth of young Hispanics and one-third of young African-Americans are unemployed.

My message today to all the people trapped in poverty is this: Politicians like Hillary Clinton have failed you.

They have used you.

You need something new. I am the only who will deliver it.

We are going to put America back to work.

We are going to put people before government.

We are going to rebuild our inner cities.

We are going to make you and your family safe, secure and prosperous.

The choice in November is a choice between a Clinton Agenda that puts Donors First—or a new agenda that puts America First.

It is a choice between a Clinton government of, by and for the powerful—or a return to government of, by and for the people.

It is a choice between certain decline, or a revival of America's promise.

The people in charge of our government say things can't change.

I am here to tell you that things <u>have to change</u>.

They want you to keep trusting the same people who've betrayed you.

I am here to tell you that if you keep supporting those who've let you down, then you will keep getting let down for the rest of your life.

I am prepared to kick the special interests out of Washington, D.C. and to hand their seat of power over to you.

It's about time.

Together, we will put the American people first again.

We will make our communities wealthy again.

We will make our cities safe again.

We will make our country strong again.

Ladies and Gentlemen: We will make America Great Again.

Donald J. Trump: Foreign Policy Speech

April 27, 2016, Washington, D.C.

Thank you for the opportunity to speak to you, and thank you to the Center for the National Interest for honoring me with this invitation.

I would like to talk today about how to develop a new foreign policy direction for our country—one that replaces randomness with purpose, ideology with strategy, and chaos with peace.

It is time to shake the rust off of America's foreign policy. It's time to invite new voices and new visions into the fold.

The direction I will outline today will also return us to a timeless principle. My foreign policy will always put the interests of the American people, and American security, above all else. That will be the foundation of every decision that I will make.

America First will be the major and overriding theme of my administration.

But to chart our path forward, we must first briefly look back.

We have a lot to be proud of. In the 1940s we saved the world. The Greatest Generation beat back the Nazis and the Japanese Imperialists.

Then we saved the world again, this time from totalitarian Communism. The Cold War lasted for decades, but we won.

Democrats and Republicans working together got Mr. Gorbachev to heed the words of President Reagan when he said: "tear down this wall."

History will not forget what we did.

Unfortunately, after the Cold War, our foreign policy veered badly off course. We failed to develop a new vision for a new time. In fact, as time went on, our foreign policy began to make less and less sense.

Logic was replaced with foolishness and arrogance, and this led to one foreign policy disaster after another.

We went from mistakes in Iraq to Egypt to Libya, to President Obama's line in the sand in Syria. Each of these actions have helped to throw the region into chaos, and gave ISIS the space it needs to grow and prosper.

It all began with the dangerous idea that we could make Western democracies out of countries that had no experience or interest in becoming a Western Democracy.

We tore up what institutions they had and then were surprised at what we unleashed. Civil war, religious fanaticism; thousands of American lives, and many trillions of dollars, were lost as a result. The vacuum was created that ISIS would fill. Iran, too, would rush in and fill the void, much to their unjust enrichment.

Our foreign policy is a complete and total disaster.

No vision, no purpose, no direction, no strategy.

Today, I want to identify five main weaknesses in our foreign policy.

FIRST, OUR RESOURCES ARE OVEREXTENDED

President Obama has weakened our military by weakening our economy. He's crippled us with wasteful spending, massive debt, low growth, a huge trade deficit and open borders.

Our manufacturing trade deficit with the world is now approaching $1 trillion a year. We're rebuilding other countries while weakening our own.

Ending the theft of American jobs will give us the resources we need to rebuild our military and regain our financial independence and strength.

I am the only person running for the Presidency who understands this problem and knows how to fix it.

SECONDLY, OUR ALLIES ARE NOT PAYING THEIR FAIR SHARE.

Our allies must contribute toward the financial, political and human costs of our tremendous security burden. But many of them are simply not doing so. They look at the United States as weak and forgiving and feel no obligation to honor their agreements with us.

In NATO, for instance, only 4 of 28 other member countries, besides America, are spending the minimum required 2% of GDP on defense.

We have spent trillions of dollars over time—on planes, missiles, ships, equipment—building up our military to provide a strong defense for Europe and Asia. The countries we are defending must pay for the cost of this defense—and, if not, the U.S. must be prepared to let these countries defend themselves.

The whole world will be safer if our allies do their part to support our common defense and security.

A Trump Administration will lead a free world that is properly armed and funded.

THIRDLY, OUR FRIENDS ARE BEGINNING TO THINK THEY CAN'T DEPEND ON US.

We've had a president who dislikes our friends and bows to our enemies.

He negotiated a disastrous deal with Iran, and then we watched them ignore its terms, even before the ink was dry.

Iran cannot be allowed to have a nuclear weapon and, under a Trump Administration, will never be allowed to have a nuclear weapon.

All of this without even mentioning the humiliation of the United States with Iran's treatment of our ten captured sailors.

In negotiation, you must be willing to walk. The Iran deal, like so many of our worst agreements, is the result of not being willing to leave the table. When the other side knows you're not going to walk, it becomes absolutely impossible to win.

At the same time, your friends need to know that you will stick by the agreements that you have with them.

President Obama gutted our missile defense program, then abandoned our missile defense plans with Poland and the Czech Republic.

He supported the ouster of a friendly regime in Egypt that had a longstanding peace treaty with Israel—and then helped bring the Muslim Brotherhood to power in its place.

Israel, our great friend and the one true Democracy in the Middle East, has been snubbed and criticized by an Administration that lacks moral clarity. Just a few days ago, Vice President Biden again criticized Israel—a force for justice and peace—for acting as an impediment to peace in the region.

President Obama has not been a friend to Israel. He has treated Iran with tender love and care and made it a great power in the Middle East—all at the expense of Israel, our other allies in the region and, critically, the United States.

We've picked fights with our oldest friends, and now they're starting to look elsewhere for help.

FOURTH, OUR RIVALS NO LONGER RESPECT US.

In fact, they are just as confused as our allies, but an even bigger problem is that they don't take us seriously any more.

When President Obama landed in Cuba on Air Force One, no leader was there to meet or greet him—perhaps an incident without precedent in the long and prestigious history of Air Force One.

Then, amazingly, the same thing happened in Saudi Arabia—it's called no respect.

Do you remember when the President made a long and expensive trip to Copenhagen, Denmark to get the Olympics for our country, and, after this unprecedented effort, it was announced that the United States came in fourth place?

He should have known the result before making such an embarrassing commitment.

The list of humiliations goes on and on.

President Obama watches helplessly as North Korea increases its aggression and expands even further with its nuclear reach.

Our president has allowed China to continue its economic assault on American jobs and wealth, refusing to enforce trade rules—or apply the leverage on China necessary to rein in North Korea.

He has even allowed China to steal government secrets with cyber-attacks and engage in industrial espionage against the United States and its companies.

We've let our rivals and challengers think they can get away with anything.

If President Obama's goal had been to weaken America, he could not have done a better job.

FINALLY, AMERICA NO LONGER HAS A CLEAR UNDERSTANDING OF OUR FOREIGN POLICY GOALS.

Since the end of the Cold War and the break-up of the Soviet Union, we've lacked a coherent foreign policy.

One day we're bombing Libya and getting rid of a dictator to foster democracy for civilians, the next day we are watching the same civilians suffer while that country falls apart.

We're a humanitarian nation. But the legacy of the Obama-Clinton interventions will be weakness, confusion, and disarray.

We have made the Middle East more unstable and chaotic than ever before.

We left Christians subject to intense persecution and even genocide.

Our actions in Iraq, Libya and Syria have helped unleash ISIS.

And we're in a war against radical Islam, but President Obama won't even name the enemy!

Hillary Clinton also refuses to say the words "radical Islam," even as she pushes for a massive increase in refugees.

After Secretary Clinton's failed intervention in Libya, Islamic terrorists in Benghazi took down our consulate and killed our ambassador and three brave Americans. Then, instead of taking charge that night, Hillary Clinton decided to go home and sleep! Incredible.

Clinton blames it all on a video, an excuse that was a total lie. Our Ambassador was murdered and our Secretary of State misled the nation—and by the way, she was not awake to take that call at 3 o'clock in the morning.

And now ISIS is making millions of dollars a week selling Libyan oil.

THIS WILL CHANGE WHEN I AM PRESIDENT.

To all our friends and allies, I say America is going to be strong again. America is going to be a reliable friend and ally again.

We're going to finally have a coherent foreign policy based upon American interests, and the shared interests of our allies.

We are getting out of the nation-building business, and instead focusing on creating stability in the world.

Our moments of greatest strength came when politics ended at the water's edge.

We need a new, rational American foreign policy, informed by the best minds and supported by both parties, as well as by our close allies.

This is how we won the Cold War, and it's how we will win our new and future struggles.

FIRST, WE NEED A LONG-TERM PLAN TO HALT THE SPREAD AND REACH OF RADICAL ISLAM.

Containing the spread of radical Islam must be a major foreign policy goal of the United States.

Events may require the use of military force. But it's also a philosophical struggle, like our long struggle in the Cold War.

In this we're going to be working very closely with our allies in the Muslim world, all of which are at risk from radical Islamic violence.

We should work together with any nation in the region that is threatened by the rise of radical Islam. But this has to be a two-way street—they must also be good to us and remember us and all we are doing for them.

The struggle against radical Islam also takes place in our homeland. There are scores of recent migrants inside our borders charged with terrorism. For every case known to the public, there are dozens more.

We must stop importing extremism through senseless immigration policies.

A pause for reassessment will help us to prevent the next San Bernardino or worse—all you have to do is look at the World Trade Center and September 11th.

And then there's ISIS. I have a simple message for them. Their days are numbered. I won't tell them where and I won't tell them how. We must as, a nation, be more unpredictable. But they're going to be gone. And soon.

SECONDLY, WE HAVE TO REBUILD OUR MILITARY AND OUR ECONOMY.

The Russians and Chinese have rapidly expanded their military capability, but look what's happened to us!

Our nuclear weapons arsenal—our ultimate deterrent—has been allowed to atrophy and is desperately in need of modernization and renewal.

Our active duty armed forces have shrunk from 2 million in 1991 to about 1.3 million today.

The Navy has shrunk from over 500 ships to 272 ships during that time.

The Air Force is about 1/3 smaller than 1991. Pilots are flying B-52s in combat missions today which are older than most people in this room.

And what are we doing about this? President Obama has proposed a 2017 defense budget that, in real dollars, cuts nearly 25% from what we were spending in 2011.

Our military is depleted, and we're asking our generals and military leaders to worry about global warming.

We will spend what we need to rebuild our military. It is the cheapest investment we can make. We will develop, build and purchase the best equipment known to mankind. Our military dominance must be unquestioned.

But we will look for savings and spend our money wisely. In this time of mounting debt, not one dollar can be wasted.

We are also going to have to change our trade, immigration and economic policies to make our economy strong again—and to put Americans first again. This will ensure that our own workers, right here in America, get the jobs and higher pay that will grow our tax revenue and increase our economic might as a nation.

We need to think smarter about areas where our technological superiority gives us an edge. This includes 3-D printing, artificial intelligence and cyber-warfare.

A great country also takes care of its warriors. Our commitment to them is absolute. A Trump Administration will give our service men and women the best equipment and support in the world when they serve, and the best care in the world when they return as veterans to civilian life.

FINALLY, WE MUST DEVELOP A FOREIGN POLICY BASED ON AMERICAN INTERESTS.

Businesses do not succeed when they lose sight of their core interests and neither do countries.

Look at what happened in the 1990s. Our embassies in Kenya and Tanzania were attacked and seventeen brave sailors were killed on the USS Cole. And what did we do? It seemed we put more effort into adding China to the World Trade Organization—which has been a disaster for the United States—than into stopping Al Qaeda.

We even had an opportunity to take out Osama Bin Laden, and didn't do it. And then, we got hit at the World Trade Center and the Pentagon, the worst attack on our country in its history.

Our foreign policy goals must be based on America's core national security interests, and the following will be my priorities.

In the Middle East, our goals must be to defeat terrorists and promote regional stability, not radical change. We need to be clear-sighted about the groups that will never be anything other than enemies.

And we must only be generous to those that prove they are our friends.

We desire to live peacefully and in friendship with Russia and China. We have serious differences with these two nations, and must regard them with open eyes. But we are not bound to be adversaries. We should seek common ground based on shared interests. Russia, for instance, has also seen the horror of Islamic terrorism.

I believe an easing of tensions and improved relations with Russia—from a position of strength—is possible. Common sense says this cycle of hostility must end. Some say the Russians won't be reasonable.

I intend to find out. If we can't make a good deal for America, then we will quickly walk from the table.

Fixing our relations with China is another important step towards a prosperous century. China respects strength, and by letting them take advantage of us economically, we have lost all of their respect. We have a massive trade deficit with China, a deficit we must find a way, quickly, to balance.

A strong and smart America is an America that will find a better friend in China. We can both benefit or we can both go our separate ways.

After I am elected President, I will also call for a summit with our NATO allies, and a separate summit with our Asian allies. In these summits, we will not only discuss a rebalancing of financial commitments, but take a fresh look at how we can adopt new strategies for tackling our common challenges.

For instance, we will discuss how we can upgrade NATO's outdated mission and structure—grown out of the Cold War—to confront our shared challenges, including migration and Islamic terrorism.

I will not hesitate to deploy military force when there is no alternative. But if America fights, it must fight to win. I will never send our finest into battle unless necessary—and will only do so if we have a plan for victory.

Our goal is peace and prosperity, not war and destruction.

The best way to achieve those goals is through a disciplined, deliberate and consistent foreign policy.

With President Obama and Secretary Clinton we've had the exact opposite: a reckless, rudderless and aimless foreign policy—one that has blazed a path of destruction in its wake.

After losing thousands of lives and spending trillions of dollars, we are in far worse shape now in the Middle East than ever before.

I challenge anyone to explain the strategic foreign policy vision of Obama-Clinton—it has been a complete and total disaster.

I will also be prepared to deploy America's economic resources. Financial leverage and sanctions can be very persuasive—but we need to use them selectively and with determination. Our power will be used if others do not play by the rules.

Our friends and enemies must know that if I draw a line in the sand, I will enforce it.

However, unlike other candidates for the presidency, war and aggression will not be my first instinct. You cannot have a foreign policy without diplomacy. A superpower understands that caution and restraint are signs of strength.

Although not in government service, I was totally against the War in Iraq, saying for many years that it would destabilize the Middle East. Sadly, I was correct, and the biggest beneficiary was Iran, who is systematically taking over Iraq and gaining access to their rich oil reserves—something it has wanted to do for decades. And now, to top it all off, we have ISIS.

My goal is to establish a foreign policy that will endure for several generations.

That is why I will also look for talented experts with new approaches, and practical ideas, rather than surrounding myself with those who have perfect resumes but very little to brag about except responsibility for a long history of failed policies and continued losses at war.

Finally, I will work with our allies to reinvigorate Western values and institutions. Instead of trying to spread "universal values" that not everyone shares, we should understand that strengthening and promoting Western civilization and its accomplishments will do more to inspire positive reforms around the world than military interventions.

THESE ARE MY GOALS, AS PRESIDENT.

I will seek a foreign policy that all Americans, whatever their party, can support, and which our friends and allies will respect and welcome.

The world must know that we do not go abroad in search of enemies, that we are always happy when old enemies become friends, and when old friends become allies.

To achieve these goals, Americans must have confidence in their country and its leadership again. Many Americans must wonder why our politicians seem more interested in defending the borders of foreign countries than their own.

Americans must know that we are putting the American people first again. On trade, on immigration, on foreign policy—the jobs, incomes and security of the American worker will always be my first priority.

No country has ever prospered that failed to put its own interests first. Both our friends and enemies put their countries above ours and we, while being fair to them, must do the same.

We will no longer surrender this country, or its people, to the false song of globalism.

The nation-state remains the true foundation for happiness and harmony. I am skeptical of international unions that tie us up and bring America down, and will never enter America into any agreement that reduces our ability to control our own affairs.

NAFTA, as an example, has been a total disaster for the U.S. and has emptied our states of our manufacturing and our jobs. Never again. Only the reverse will happen. We will keep our jobs and bring in new ones. There will be consequences for companies that leave the U.S. only to exploit it later.

Under a Trump Administration, no American citizen will ever again feel that their needs come second to the citizens of foreign countries.

I will view the world through the clear lens of American interests.

I will be America's greatest defender and most loyal champion. We will not apologize for becoming successful again, but will instead embrace the unique heritage that makes us who we are.

The world is most peaceful, and most prosperous, when America is strongest.

America will continually play the role of peacemaker.

We will always help to save lives and, indeed, humanity itself. But to play that role, we must make America strong again.

We must make America respected again. And we must make America great again.

If we do that, perhaps this century can be the most peaceful and prosperous the world has ever known. Thank you.

APPENDIX 5

Donald J. Trump: Speech on Stakes of the Election

June 22, 2016, New York City, New York

Today I'd like to share my thoughts about the stakes in this election.

People have asked me why I am running for President.

I have built an amazing business that I love and I get to work side-by-side with my children every day.

We come to work together and turn visions into reality.

We think big, and then we make it happen.

I love what I do, and I am grateful beyond words to the nation that has allowed me to do it.

So when people ask me why I am running, I quickly answer: I am running to give back to this country which has been so good to me.

When I see the crumbling roads and bridges, or the dilapidated airports, or the factories moving overseas to Mexico, or to other countries, I know these problems can all be fixed, but not by Hillary Clinton—only by me.

The fact is, we can come back bigger and better and stronger than ever before—Jobs, jobs, jobs!

Everywhere I look, I see the possibilities of what our country could be. But we can't solve any of these problems by relying on the politicians who created them.

We will never be able to fix a rigged system by counting on the same people who rigged it in the first place.

The insiders wrote the rules of the game to keep themselves in power and in the money.

That's why we're asking Bernie Sanders' voters to join our movement: so together we can fix the system for ALL Americans. Importantly, this includes fixing all of our many disastrous trade deals.

Because it's not just the political system that's rigged. It's the whole economy.

It's rigged by big donors who want to keep down wages.

It's rigged by big businesses who want to leave our country, fire our workers, and sell their products back into the U.S. with absolutely no consequences for them.

It's rigged by bureaucrats who are trapping kids in failing schools.

It's rigged against you, the American people.

Hillary Clinton who, as most people know, is a world class liar—just look at her pathetic email and server statements, or her phony landing in Bosnia where she said she was under attack but the attack turned out to be young girls handing her flowers, a total self-serving lie.

Brian Williams' career was destroyed for saying far less.

Yesterday, she even tried to attack me and my many businesses. But here is the bottom line: I started off in Brooklyn New York, not so long ago, with a small loan and built a business worth over 10 billion dollars. I have always had a talent for building businesses and, importantly, creating jobs. That is a talent our country desperately needs.

I am running for President to end the unfairness and to put you, the American worker, first.

We are going to put America First, and we are going to Make America Great again.

This election will decide whether we are ruled by the people, or by the politicians.

Here is my promise to the American voter:

If I am elected President, I will end the special interest monopoly in Washington, D.C.

The other candidate in this race has spent her entire life making money for special interests—and taking money from special interests.

Hillary Clinton has perfected the politics of personal profit and theft.

She ran the State Department like her own personal hedge fund—doing favors for oppressive regimes, and many others, in exchange for cash.

Then, when she left, she made $21.6 million giving speeches to Wall Street banks and other special interests—in less than 2 years—secret speeches that she does not want to reveal to the public.

Together, she and Bill made $153 million giving speeches to lobbyists, CEOs, and foreign governments in the years since 2001.

They totally own her, and that will never change.

The choice in this election is a choice between taking our government back from the special interests, or surrendering our last scrap of independence to their total and complete control.

Those are the stakes.

Hillary Clinton wants to be President. But she doesn't have the temperament, or, as Bernie Sanders' said, the judgement, to be president.

She believes she is entitled to the office.

Her campaign slogan is "I'm with her."

You know what my response to that is? I'm with you: the American people.

She thinks it's all about her.

I know it's all about you—I know it's all about making America Great Again for All Americans.

Our country lost its way when we stopped putting the American people first.

We got here because we switched from a policy of Americanism—focusing on what's good for America's middle class—to a policy of globalism, focusing on how to make money for large corporations who can move their wealth and workers to foreign countries all to the detriment of the American worker and the American economy.

We reward companies for offshoring, and we punish companies for doing business in America and keeping our workers employed.

This is not a rising tide that lifts all boats.

This is a wave of globalization that wipes out our middle class and our jobs.

We need to reform our economic system so that, once again, we can all succeed together, and America can become rich again.

That's what we mean by America First.

Our country will be better off when we start making our own products again, bringing our once great manufacturing capabilities back to our shores.

Our Founders understood this.

One of the first major bills signed by George Washington called for "the encouragement and protection of manufactur[ing]" in America.

Our first Republican President, Abraham Lincoln, warned us by saying:

"The abandonment of the protective policy by the American government will produce want and ruin among our people."

I have visited the cities and towns across America and seen the devastation caused by the trade policies of Bill and Hillary Clinton.

Hillary Clinton supported Bill Clinton's disastrous NAFTA, just like she supported China's entrance into the World Trade Organization.

We've lost nearly one-third of our manufacturing jobs since these two Hillary-backed agreements were signed.

Our trade deficit with China soared 40% during Hillary Clinton's time as Secretary of State—a disgraceful performance for which she should not be congratulated, but rather scorned.

Then she let China steal hundreds of billions of dollars in our intellectual property—a crime which is continuing to this day.

Hillary Clinton gave China millions of our best jobs, and effectively let China completely rebuild itself.

In return, Hillary Clinton got rich!

The book Clinton Cash, by Peter Schweitzer, documents how Bill and Hillary used the State Department to enrich their family at America's expense.

She gets rich making you poor.

Here is a quote from the book: "At the center of US policy toward China was Hillary Clinton…at this critical time for US-China relations, Bill Clinton gave a number of speeches that were underwritten by the Chinese government and its supporters."

These funds were paid to the Clinton bank account while Hillary was negotiating with China on behalf of the United States.

She sold out our workers, and our country, for Beijing.

Hillary Clinton has also been the biggest promoter of the Trans-Pacific Partnership, which will ship millions more of our jobs overseas—and give up Congressional power to an international foreign commission.

Now, because I have pointed out why it would be such a disastrous deal, she is pretending that she is against it. She has even deleted this record of total support from her book—deletion is something she is very good at—(at least 30,000 emails are missing.)

But this latest Clinton cover-up doesn't change anything: if she is elected president, she will adopt the Trans-Pacific Partnership, and we will lose millions of jobs and our economic independence for good. She will do this, just as she has betrayed the American worker on trade at every single stage of her career—and it will be even worse than the Clintons' NAFTA deal.

I want trade deals, but they have to be great for the United States and our workers.

We don't make great deals anymore, but we will once I become president.

It's not just our economy that's been corrupted, but our foreign policy too.

The Hillary Clinton foreign policy has cost America thousands of lives and trillions of dollars—and unleashed ISIS across the world.

No Secretary of State has been more wrong, more often, and in more places than Hillary Clinton.

Her decisions spread death, destruction and terrorism everywhere she touched.

Among the victims is our late Ambassador, Chris Stevens. He was left helpless to die as Hillary Clinton soundly slept in her bed—that's right, when the phone rang at 3 o'clock in the morning, she was sleeping.

Ambassador Stevens and his staff in Libya made hundreds of requests for security.

Hillary Clinton's State Department refused them all.

She started the war that put him in Libya, denied him the security he asked for, then left him there to die.

To cover her tracks, Hillary lied about a video being the cause of his death.

Here is what one of the victim's mothers had to say:

"I want the whole world to know it: she lied to my face, and you don't want this person to be president."

In 2009, before Hillary Clinton was sworn in, it was a different world.

Libya was cooperating.

Iraq was seeing a reduction in violence.

Syria was under control.

Iran was being choked by sanctions.

Egypt was governed by a friendly regime that honored its peace treaty with Israel.

ISIS wasn't even on the map.

Fast forward to 2013: In just four years, Secretary Clinton managed to almost single-handedly destabilize the entire Middle East.

Her invasion of Libya handed the country over to the ISIS barbarians.

Thanks to Hillary Clinton, Iran is now the dominant Islamic power in the Middle East, and on the road to nuclear weapons.

Hillary Clinton's support for violent regime change in Syria has thrown the country into one of the bloodiest civil wars anyone has ever seen—while giving ISIS a launching pad for terrorism against the West.

She helped force out a friendly regime in Egypt and replace it with the radical Muslim Brotherhood. The Egyptian military has retaken control, but Clinton has opened the Pandora's Box of radical Islam.

Then, there was the disastrous strategy of announcing our departure date from Iraq, handing large parts of the country over to ISIS killers.

ISIS threatens us today because of the decisions Hillary Clinton has made.

ISIS also threatens peaceful Muslims across the Middle East, and peaceful Muslims across the world, who have been terribly victimized by horrible brutality—and who only want to raise their kids in peace and safety.

In short, Hillary Clinton's tryout for the presidency has produced one deadly foreign policy disaster after another.

It all started with her bad judgment in supporting the War in Iraq in the first place.

Though I was not in government service, I was among the earliest to criticize the rush to war, and yes, even before the war ever started.

But Hillary Clinton learned nothing from Iraq, because when she got into power she couldn't wait to rush us off to war in Libya.

She lacks the temperament, the judgment and the competence to lead.

In the words of a Secret Service agent posted outside the Oval Office:

"She simply lacks the integrity and temperament to serve in the office... from the bottom of my soul, I know this to be true... Her leadership style—volcanic, impulsive... disdainful of the rules set for everyone else—hasn't changed a bit."

Perhaps the most terrifying thing about Hillary Clinton's foreign policy is that she refuses to acknowledge the threat posed by Radical Islam.

In fact, Hillary Clinton supports a radical 550% increase in Syrian refugees coming into the United States, and that's an increase over President Obama's already very high number.

Under her plan, we would admit hundreds of thousands of refugees from the most dangerous countries on Earth—with no way to screen who they are or what they believe.

Already, hundreds of recent immigrants and their children have been convicted of terrorist activity inside the U.S.

The father of the Orlando shooter was a Taliban supporter from Afghanistan, one of the most repressive anti-gay and anti-women regimes on Earth.

I only want to admit people who share our values and love our people.

Hillary Clinton wants to bring in people who believe women should be enslaved and gays put to death.

Maybe her motivation lies among the more than 1,000 foreign donations Hillary failed to disclose while at the State Department.

Hillary Clinton may be the most corrupt person ever to seek the presidency.

Here is some more of what we learned from the book,

Clinton Cash:

A foreign telecom giant faced possible State Department sanctions for providing technology to Iran, and other oppressive regimes. So what did this company do? For the first time ever, they decided to pay Bill Clinton $750,000 for a single speech. The Clintons got their cash, the telecom company escaped sanctions.

Hillary Clinton's State Department approved the transfer of 20% of America's uranium holdings to

Russia, while 9 investors in the deal funneled $145 million to the Clinton Foundation.

Hillary Clinton appointed a top donor to a national security board with top secret access—even though he had no national security credentials.

Hillary Clinton accepted $58,000 in jewelry from the government of Brunei when she was Secretary of State—plus millions more for her foundation. The Sultan of Brunei has pushed oppressive Sharia law, including the punishment of death by stoning for being gay. The government of Brunei also stands to be one of the biggest beneficiaries of Hillary's Trans-Pacific Partnership, which she would absolutely approve if given the chance.

Hillary Clinton took up to $25 million from Saudi Arabia, where being gay is also punishable by death.

Hillary took millions from Kuwait, Qatar, Oman and many other countries that horribly abuse women and LGBT citizens.

To cover-up her corrupt dealings, Hillary Clinton illegally stashed her State Department emails on a private server.

Her server was easily hacked by foreign governments—perhaps even by her financial backers in Communist China—putting all of America in danger.

Then there are the 33,000 emails she deleted.

While we may not know what is in those deleted emails, our enemies probably do.

So they probably now have a blackmail file over someone who wants to be President of the United States.

This fact alone disqualifies her from the Presidency.

We can't hand over our government to someone whose deepest, darkest secrets may be in the hands of our enemies.

National security is also immigration security—and Hillary wants neither.

Hillary Clinton has put forward the most radical immigration platform in the history of the United States.

She has pledged to grant mass amnesty and in her first 100 days, end virtually all immigration enforcement, and thus create totally open borders in the United States.

The first victims of her radical policies will be poor African-American and Hispanic workers who need jobs. They are the ones she will hurt the most.

Let me share with you a letter our campaign received from Mary Ann Mendoza.

She lost her amazing son, Police Sergeant Brandon Mendoza, after he was killed by an illegal immigrant because of the open borders policies supported by Hillary Clinton.

Sadly, the Mendoza family is just one of thousands who have suffered the same fate.

Here is an excerpt from Mrs. Mendoza's letter:

"Hillary Clinton, who already has the blood of so many on her hands, is now announcing that she is willing to put each and every one of our lives in harms' way—an open door policy to criminals and terrorists to enter our country. Hillary is not concerned about you or I, she is only concerned about the power the presidency would bring to her. She needs to go to prison to pay for the crimes she has already committed against this country."

Hillary also wants to spend hundreds of billions to resettle Middle Eastern refugees in the United States, on top of the current record level of immigration.

For the amount of money Hillary Clinton would like to spend on refugees, we could rebuild every inner city in America.

Hillary's Wall Street immigration agenda will keep immigrant communities poor, and unemployed Americans out of work. She can't claim to care about African-American and Hispanic workers when she wants to bring in millions of new low-wage workers to compete against them.

Here are a few things a Trump Administration will do for America in the first 100 days:

Appoint judges who will uphold the Constitution. Hillary Clinton's radical judges will virtually abolish the 2nd Amendment.

Change immigration rules to give unemployed Americans an opportunity to fill good-paying jobs.

Stand up to countries that cheat on trade, of which there are many.

Cancel rules and regulations that send jobs overseas.

Lift restrictions on energy production.

Repeal and replace job-killing Obamacare—it is a disaster.

Pass massive tax reform to create millions of new jobs.

Impose tough new ethics rules to restore dignity to the Office of Secretary of State.

There is one common theme in all of these reforms.

It's going to be America First.

This is why the stakes in November are so great.

On election day, the politicians stand trial before the people.

The voters are the jury. Their ballots are the verdict. We don't need or want another Clinton or Obama.

Come November, the American people will have a chance to issue a verdict on the politicians that have sacrificed their security, betrayed their prosperity, and sold out their country.

They will have a chance to vote for a new agenda with big dreams, bold ideas and enormous possibilities for the American people.

Hillary Clinton's message is old and tired. Her message is that can't change.

My message is that things have to change—and this is our one chance do it. This is our last chance to do it.

Americans are the people that tamed the West, that dug out the Panama Canal, that sent satellites across the solar system, that built the great dams, and so much more.

Then we started thinking small.

We stopped believing in what America could do, and became reliant on other countries, other people, and other institutions.

We lost our sense of purpose, and daring.

But that's not who we are.

Come this November, we can bring America back—bigger and better, and stronger than ever.

We will build the greatest infrastructure on the planet earth—the roads and railways and airports of tomorrow.

Our military will have the best technology and finest equipment—we will bring it back all the way.

Massive new factories will come roaring into our country—breathing life and hope into our communities.

Inner cities, which have been horribly abused by Hillary Clinton and the Democrat Party, will finally be rebuilt.

Construction is what I know—nobody knows it better.

The real wages for our workers have not been raised for 18 years—but these wages will start going up, along with the new jobs. Hillary's massive taxation, regulation and open borders will destroy jobs and drive down wages for everyone.

We are also going to be supporting our police and law enforcement—we can never forget the great job they do.

I am also going to appoint great Supreme Court Justices.

Our country is going to start working again.

People are going to start working again.

Parents are going to start dreaming big for their children again—including parents in our inner cities.

Americans are going to start believing in the future or our country.

We are going to make America rich again.

We are going to make America safe again.

We are going to make America Great Again—and Great Again For EVERYONE.

APPENDIX 6

Phyllis Schlafly's Writings about Donald Trump

PHYLLIS SCHLAFLY'S WEEKLY COLUMN

1. May 12, 2015, Let's Get On a Pro-American Track, http://www.eagleforum.org/publications/column/lets-get-on-a-pro-american-track.html.

2. July 7, 2015, Don't Give Obama More Power Over Schools, http://www.eagleforum.org/publications/column/dont-give-obama-more-power-over-schools.html.

3.   July 14, 2015, Donald Trump Shakes
      Up the 2016 Campaign, http://www.
      eagleforum.org/publications/column/
      donald-trump-shakes-up-the-2016-
      campaign.html.

4.   July 28, 2015, The Sanctuary Scandal,
      http://www.eagleforum.org/
      publications/column/the-sanctuary-
      scandal.html.

5.   August 18, 2015, Donald Drives the
      Debate, http://www.eagleforum.org/
      publications/column/donald-drives-
      the-debate.html.

6.   September 1, 2015, Anchor Babies on
      Trial in Texas, http://www.
      eagleforum.org/publications/column/
      anchor-babies-on-trial-in-texas.html.

7.   September 22, 2015, Congress Must
      Exercise Its Power of the Purse, http://
      www.eagleforum.org/publications/
      column/congress-must-exercise-its-
      power-of-the-purse.html.

8.   October 6, 2015, The Establishment
      Looks for a New Plan B, http://www.
      eagleforum.org/publications/column/
      the-establishment-looks-for-a-new-
      plan-b.html.

9. November 24, 2015, Governors Say "Not in My State!," http://www.eagleforum.org/publications/column/governors-say-not-in-my-state.html.

10. December 15, 2015, Donald Trump Channels Pat McCarran, http://www.eagleforum.org/publications/column/donald-trump-channels-pat-mccarran.html.

11. December 22, 2015, Ryan Leads Republicans to Defeat, http://www.eagleforum.org/publications/column/ryan-leads-republicans-defeat.html.

12. January 19, 2016, Will the Republican Establishment Stand Down?, http://www.eagleforum.org/publications/column/will-republican-establishment-stand.html.

13. February 2, 2016, America's "Last Chance," http://www.eagleforum.org/publications/column/americas-last-chance.html.

14. February 23, 2016, How Common Core Ended the Bush Dynasty, http://www.eagleforum.org/publications/column/common-core-ended-bush-dynasty.html.

15. March 8, 2016, Republicans Debate
    Guest Workers, http://www.
    eagleforum.org/publications/column/
    republicans-debate-guest-workers.
    html.
16. March 15, 2016, Candidates Turn
    Against Trade Deals, http://www.
    eagleforum.org/publications/column/
    candidates-turn-against-trade-deals.
    html.
17. April 26, 2016, Obama's Legacy Tour,
    http://www.eagleforum.org/
    publications/column/obamas-legacy-
    tour.html.
18. May 10, 2016, No Third-Party
    Candidate, http://www.eagleforum.
    org/publications/column/failed-
    republicans-want-to-rewrite-the-
    constitution.html.
19. June 7, 2016, Put the Wall in the
    Platform, http://www.eagleforum.org/
    publications/column/put-the-wall-in-
    the-platform.html.
20. June 14, 2016, Congress Is Close to
    Drafting Our Daughters, http://www.
    eagleforum.org/publications/column/
    congress-is-close-to-drafting-our-
    daughters.html.

21. June 28, 2016, Brexit Stuns the
    Globalists, http://www.eagleforum.
    org/publications/column/brexit-stuns-
    the-globalists.html.

22. July 5, 2016, Trump's Muslim Ban
    Gains Support, http://www.eagleforum.
    org/publications/column/trumps-
    muslim-ban-gains-support.html.

23. July 12, 2016, Trump Battles Globalist
    Republicans, http://www.eagleforum.
    org/publications/column/trump-
    battles-globalist-republicans.html.

24. July 19, 2016, How Pence
    Complements Trump, http://www.
    eagleforum.org/publications/column/
    how-pence-complements-trump.html.

PHYLLIS SCHLAFLY REPORT

1. May 2015, Let's Get on a Pro-American
   Track, http://www.eagleforum.org/
   publications/column/lets-get-on-a-pro-
   american-track.html.

2. July 2015, Don't Give Obama More
   Power Over Schools, http://www.
   eagleforum.org/publications/psr/
   july15.html.

3. September 2015, "Anchor Babies" on Trial, http://www.eagleforum.org/publications/psr/sept15.html.

4. October 2015, The Establishment Looks for "Plan B," http://www.eagleforum.org/publications/psr/oct15.html.

5. November 2015, Donald Drives the Debate, http://www.eagleforum.org/publications/psr/nov15.html.

6. December 2015, Governors Say "Not in My State!," http://www.eagleforum.org/publications/psr/dec15.html.

7. February 2016, America's "Last Chance," http://www.eagleforum.org/publications/psr/feb16.html.

8. March 2016, "What We Learned from the Debates," http://www.eagleforum.org/publications/psr/mar16.html.

9. May 2016, "Trump and Reagan: Similarities and Differences," http://www.eagleforum.org/publications/psr/may16.html.

10. June 2016, Put the Wall in the Platform, http://www.eagleforum.org/publications/column/put-the-wall-in-the-platform.html.

PHYLLIS SCHLAFLY 3 MINUTE RADIO COMMENTARIES

1. September 14, 2015, Trump Shakes Up the 2016 Campaign, http://blog.eagleforum.org/2015/09/trump-shakes-up-2016-campaign.html#more.
2. September 18, 2015, Sanctuary for Illegals but Not Americans, http://blog.eagleforum.org/2015/09/sanctuary-for-illegals-but-not-americans.html#more.
3. September 23, 2015, 2016 Candidates and Education, http://blog.eagleforum.org/2015/09/2016-candidates-and-education.html#more.
4. September 28, 2015, Real Cases of Illegal Immigrant Crimes, http://blog.eagleforum.org/2015/09/real-cases-of-illegal-immigrant-crimes.html#more.
5. October 7, 2015, Trump Makes Immigration a Big Issue, http://blog.eagleforum.org/2015/10/trump-makes-immigration-big-issue.html#more.

6.   October 8, 2015, Trump Promises
      Immigration Crackdown, http://blog.
      eagleforum.org/2015/10/trump-
      promises-immigration-crackdown.
      html#more.

7.   November 6, 2015, Congress Must
      Exercise Its Power of the Purse, http://
      blog.eagleforum.org/2015/11/congress-
      must-exercise-its-power-of.html#more.

8.   December 2, 2015, Establishment
      Candidates Don't Connect, http://
      blog.eagleforum.org/2015/12/
      establishment-candidates-dont-
      connect.html#more.

9.   January 19, 2015, Hispanic
      Americans Oppose Illegal
      Immigrants, http://blog.eagleforum.
      org/2016/01/hispanic-americans-
      oppose-illegal.html#more.

10.   January 25, 2016, Keeping Track of
      Refugees, http://blog.eagleforum.
      org/2016/01/keeping-track-of-
      refugees.html#more.

11.   February 1, 2016, Donald Trump's
      Constitutional Moratorium, http://
      blog.eagleforum.org/2016/02/donald-
      trumps-constitutional-moratorium.
      html#more.

12. February 2, 2016, Donald Trump Channels Pat McCarran, http://blog. eagleforum.org/2016/02/donald-trump-channels-pat-mccarran.html#more.

13. February 3, 2016, Ryan Leads Republicans to Defeat, http://blog. eagleforum.org/2016/02/ryan-leads-republicans-to-defeat.html#more.

14. March 1, 2016, Will the Republican Establishment Stand Down?, http://blog. eagleforum.org/2016/03/will-republican-establishment-stand-down.html#more.

15. March 2, 2016, Kingmaker's Plot to Steal the Nomination, http://blog. eagleforum.org/2016/03/kingmakers-plot-to-steal-nomination.html#more.

16. March 7, 2016, 500,000 Visa Overstays in 2015, http://blog. eagleforum.org/2016/03/500000-visa-overstays-in-2015.html#more.

17. April 15, 2016, Harm of Free Trade Revealed, http://blog.eagleforum. org/2016/04/harm-of-free-trade-revealed.html#more.

18. May 2, 2016, Republicans Debate Guest Workers, http://blog. eagleforum.org/2016/05/republicans-debate-guest-workers.html#more.

19. May 9, 2016, Candidates Turn Against Trade Deals, http://blog.eagleforum.org/2016/05/candidates-turn-against-trade-deals.html#more.

20. May 10, 2016, Tariffs on Chinese Goods, http://blog.eagleforum.org/2016/05/tariffs-on-chinese-goods.html#more.

21. May 26, 2016, Illegals Hired Instead of Americans, http://blog.eagleforum.org/2016/05/illegals-hired-instead-of-americans.html.

22. June 7, 2016, Paris Climate Agreement to Bypass Senate, http://blog.eagleforum.org/2016/06/paris-climate-agreement-to-bypass-senate.html.

23. June 10, 2016, Another American Killed by Criminal Alien, http://blog.eagleforum.org/2016/06/another-american-killed-by-criminal.html.

24. July 8, 2016, The Same Old Con (not posted yet).

25. July 15, 2016, Sessions Shoots Straight on Hillary (not posted yet).

26. July 18, 2016, Third-Party Candidate Issue (not posted yet).

27. July 19, 2016, Why Evangelicals Should Support Trump (not posted yet).
28. August 3, 2016, Put a Wall in the Platform (not posted yet).
29. August 4, 2016, Platform Fight Brewing on Immigration (not posted yet).
30. August 5, 2016, Brexit Vote, Trump, Echo Reagan Elections (not posted yet).
31. August 9, 2016, Trump Contrasts the Bush Globalist Tradition (not posted yet).
32. August 23, 2016, Why We Need a Tough President (not posted yet).
33. August 29, 2016, Learning from Tragedy (not posted yet).

Notes

INTRODUCTION

1. See www.HillaryClinton.com for her campaign website, @HillaryClinton on Twitter, and Hillary Clinton on Facebook.
2. Jennifer Epstein, "Hillary Clinton Comes Out Against Keystone Pipeline," *Bloomberg*, September 22, 2015.
3. Mark Antonio Wright, "Hillary: I'll Put Coal Miners and Coal Companies 'Out of Business,'" *National Review*, March 14, 2016.
4. John Binder, "Liberal Heads Explode as Pat Buchanan Flawlessly Explains Trump's Unprecedented Rise to the Top," *BizPac Review*, May 5, 2016.
5. Peter Morici, "How to Fix Free Trade," Fox News, April 26, 2016.
6. Rebecca Kaplan, "Hillary Clinton: U.S. Should Take More Syrian Refugees," CBS News, September 20, 2015.

7. Jan C. Ting, "Court Rulings Support Trump's Muslim Immigration Plan," *Philadelphia Inquirer*, December 11, 2015.
8. Brian O'Connell, "Donald Trump's Social Security Plan Makes a Lot of Sense," TheStreet, February 20, 2016.
9. Donald J. Trump, *Time to Get Tough: Making America #1 Again* (Washington: Regnery Publishing, Inc., 2011).

CHAPTER 1
1. Otis L. Graham, Jr, "Tracing Liberal Woes to the '65 Immigration Act," *Christian Science Monitor*, December 1995.
2. Caroline May, "Poll: 61 Percent Say Immigration 'Jeopardizes the United States,'" Breitbart News, March 7, 2016.
3. Donald J. Trump, *Crippled America: How to Make America Great Again* (New York: Threshold, 2015).
4. Donald J. Trump, "Immigration Reform That Will Make America Great Again," TRUMP, https://www.donaldjtrump.com/positions/immigration-reform.
5. Jake Miller, "Donald Trump Defends Calling Mexican Immigrants 'Rapists,'" CBS News, July 2, 2015.
6. Caroline May, "Illegal Immigrants Accounted for Nearly 37 Percent of Federal Sentences in FY 2014," Breitbart News, July 7, 2015.
7. Joel B. Pollack, "Family of Murdered Woman Sues San Francisco Over 'Sanctuary City' Policy," Breitbart, May 27, 2016.
8. Eliott C. McLaughlin, "Chief Blames Immigration Policy in Woman's Murder," CNN, August 10, 2015.
9. Jessica Glenza, "Native American Family Attacked in Deadly Shooting on Montana Highway," *Guardian*, July 31, 2015.
10. Donald J. Trump, *Crippled America: How to Make America Great Again* (New York: Threshold, 2015).
11. Bryan Griffith, Jessica Vaughan, and Marguerite Telford, "Map: Sanctuary Cities, Counties, and States," Center for Immigration Studies, March 3, 2016.

12. Jessica Vaughan, "Deportation Numbers Unwrapped," Center for Immigration Studies, October 2013.
13. Greg Hilburn, "Sanctuary Cities Bill Runs Into Roadblock," *News Star*, May 17, 2016.
14. Alan Gomez, "States Are Cracking Down on 'Sanctuary Cities,'" *USA Today*, October 15, 2015.
15. Jon Feere, "Birth Tourists Come from Around the Globe," Center for Immigration Studies, August 26, 2015.
16. Donald J. Trump, *Crippled America: How to Make America Great Again* (New York: Threshold, 2015).
17. Allan Wall, "Mexico Files Amicus Brief in Texas Anchor Baby Case," VDARE, August 27, 2015.
18. William C. Triplett II, "If Trump Wins, the Drug Cartels Lose," *Washington Times*, July 3, 2016.
19. Patrick J. Buchanan, *The Death of the West: How Dying Populations and Immigrant Invasions Imperil Our Country and Civilization* (New York: Thomas Dunne Books, 2002).
20. Donald J. Trump, *Time to Get Tough: Making America #1 Again* (Washington: Regnery Publishing, Inc., 2011).

CHAPTER 2
1. Marilyn Geewax, "Moving Air-Conditioning Jobs to Mexico Becomes Hot Campaign Issue," *NPR*, March 14, 2016.
2. Donald J. Trump, *Time to Get Tough: Making America #1 Again* (Washington: Regnery Publishing, Inc., 2011).
3. Stephan Manning and Marcus M. Larsen, "Trump and Clinton Want to Bring Back Millions of Outsourced Jobs – Here's Why They Can't," WRAL, May 18, 2016.
4. Micah Maidenberg, "This Time Trump May Be Right," *Crain's Chicago Business*, May 21, 2016.
5. Carmen DeNavas-Walt and Bernadette D. Proctor, "Income and Poverty in the United State: 2014," U.S. Census Bureau, September 2015.
6. "Vietnam," *The World Bank*, http://data.worldbank.org/country/vietnam.

7. Halimah Abdullah and Frank Thorp V, "Senate Approves 'Fast Track' Trade Authority in Win for Obama," MSNBC, June 24, 2015.

8. Phyllis Schlafly, "Let's Get On a Pro-American Track," *EagleForum*, May 13, 2015.

9. Jared Bernstein, "Big Report, Little Finding: The ITC Evaluates the Economic Impact of the TPP," *Huffington Post*, May 20, 2016.

10. Robert E. Scott, "ITC Study Shows Minimal benefits and Downplays Potentially High Costs of Trans-Pacific Partnership," Economic Policy Institute, May 19, 2016.

11. Ibid.

12. Ibid.

13. Paola Masman, "U.S.-Korea Trade Deal Resulted in Growing Trade Deficits and More Than 95,000 Lost U.S. Jobs," Coalition for a Prosperous America, May 5, 2016.

14. "KORUS: Another NAFTA-Like Trade Deal," *Economy in Crisis*.

15. Donald J. Trump, *Crippled America: How to Make America Great Again* (New York: Threshold, 2015).

16. Robert E. Scott, "ITC Study Shows Minimal benefits and Downplays Potentially High Costs of Trans-Pacific Partnership," Economic Policy Institute, May 19, 2016.

17. Steve Brachmann, "South Korean Car Makers to Increase Their Market Share In Coming Years" *IPWatchdog*, June 8, 2015.

18. Leo Hindery, Jr., "As Free Trade Pacts Expand, U.S. Trade Deficit Soars. Why Add More?," Reuters, February 17, 2015.

19. "U.S. Polling Shows Strong Opposition to More of the Same U.S. Trade Deals from Independents, Republicans, and Democrats Alike," *Public Citizen*, July 2015.

20. Lawrence Mishel, et al., "The State of Working America," https://stateofworkingamerica.org/files/book/Chapter2-Income.pdf.

21.   Walter Block, Robert W. McGee, and Kristi Spissinger,
       "No Policy Is Good Policy: A Radical Proposal for U.S.
       Industrial Policy," *Glendale Law Review.*
22.   Daniel J. Ikenson, "Beyond the American
       Manufacturing Competitiveness Act: Congress Should
       Get More Serious About Tariff Reform," Cato Institute,
       April 26, 2016.
23.   Donald J. Trump, *The America We Deserve*, (New
       York: Renaissance Books, 2000).
24.   Brett M. Decker, "Five Questions with Donald Trump,"
       Washington Times: October 15, 2012.
25.   Donald J Trump, "Reforming the U.S.-China Trade
       Relationship to Make America Great Again," TRUMP,
       https://www.donaldjtrump.com/positions/us-china-
       trade-reform.
26.   Patrick J. Buchanan, *The Great Betrayal: How
       American Sovereignty and Social Justice Are Being
       Sacrificed to the Gods of the Global Economy* (New
       York: Little, Brown and Company, 1998).
27.   James S. Robbins, "Hillary Clinton's Real Trans-Pacific
       Partnership Views Shrouded by Self-Interest," USA
       Today, October 7, 2015.
28.   "U.S. Polling Shows Strong Opposition to More of the
       Same U.S. Trade Deals from Independents, Republicans,
       and Democrats Alike," *Public Citizen*, July 2015.
29.   Donald J. Trump, *Crippled America: How To Make
       America Great Again*, (New York: Threshold, 2015).

CHAPTER 3
1.   Jeffrey Lord, *What America Needs* (Washington:
       Regnery Publishing, Inc., 2016).
2.   "79% See Political Correctness As Serious Problem in
       America," *Rasmussen Reports*, November 2, 2011.
3.   Stephen Moore, "The Stupid Party Keeps Getting
       Stupider," *American Spectator*, June 10, 2016.
4.   Paul Bedard, "Poll: 27% of Democrats Want 'Global
       Warming' Foes Prosecuted by Feds," *Washington
       Examiner*, November 12, 2015.

5. Michael Bastasch, "Dem Congressmen: First Amendment Doesn't Protect Global Warming Skeptics," *Daily Caller*, June 13, 2016.

6. Mark J. Fitzgibbons, "AG Claude Walker Contradicts Self on 'Danger' of Fossil Fuels," *American Thinker*, April 20, 2016.

7. Larry Bell, "Climategate Star Michael Mann Courts Legal Disaster," *Forbes*, September 18, 2012.

8. Donald J. Trump, Twitter post, January 1, 2014, 4:39 p.m., https://twitter.com/realdonaldtrump/status/4185 42137899491328?lang=en.

9. Donald J. Trump, "Trump: Clinton Can't Protect LGBT Community While Importing Those Who Want To Oppress Them," RealClear Politics, June 13, 2016.

10. Jamie Schram and Tina Moore, "Gunman Pledged Allegiance to ISIS Before Florida Gay Club Massacre," *New York Post*, June 12, 2016.

11. Allum Bokhari, "Facebook Deletes Pamela Geller's 'Stop Islamization of America' Page After Orlando Attack," Breitbart News, June 12, 2016.

12. Tom Ciccotta, "Twitter Appears to Censor Popular #GaysForTrump Hashtag," Breitbart News, June 15, 2016.

13. Barack Obama, "Remarks by the President on Mass Shooting in Orlando," White House, Washington, D.C., June 12, 2016.

14. Blake Neff, "San Jose Mayor: Trump To Blame For Protestor Riots," Daily Caller, June 3, 2016.

15. Heather Wilhelm, "America's Hapless Terror Whodunit," RealClear Politics, June 16, 2016.

16. Bill Donohue, "Christians Blamed For Muslim Murders," http://www.catholicleague.org/wp-content/uploads/2016/06/CHRISTIANS-BLAMED-FOR-MUSLIM-MURDERS-NR.pdf.

17. David Martosko, "He Was More Angry at Me Than He Was at the Shooter," *Daily Mail,* June 15, 2016.

18. Saul D. Alinsky, *Rules for Radicals* (New York: Random House, 1971).

19. Russell Kirk, *The Conservative Mind: From Burke to Eliot*, (Washington, D.C.: Regnery Books, 1987), 8.

20. Charles J. Chaput, "Homily for Mass Before March for Life," *CatholicPhilly.com*, January 22, 2014.

21. Ibid.

22. Rich Lowry, "Behold the Cultural Power of the Left," *National Review*, June 23, 2015.

23. Jeffrey Lord, *What America Needs*, (Washington D.C.: Regnery Publishing, Inc., 2016).

CHAPTER 4

1. Colin Campbell, "Trump: Antonin Scalia was 'One of the Best of All Time,'" *Business Insider*, February 13, 2016.

2. Jenna Johnson and Robert Barnes, "Trump Releases List of 11 Judges He'd Consider Nominating to Supreme Court," *Washington Post,* May 18, 2016.

3. Donald J. Trump, "Donald J. Trump Releases List of Potential United States Supreme Court Justices," TRUMP, May 18, 2016.

4. Tom Strode, "Trump's Supreme Court List Draws Mixed Reaction," *Baptist Press*, May 19, 2016.

5. "Trump's Supreme Court List a 'Conservative Goldmine,'" Breitbart News, May 21, 2016.

6. Newt Gingrich, *A Nation Like No Other: Why American Exceptionalism Matters* (Washington, D.C.: Regnery Publishing, Inc., 2011).

7. "Cases of Judicial Activism," Heritage Foundation, http://www.heritage.org/initiatives/rule-of-law/judicial-activism.

8. Chris Stigal, "Judicial Crisis Network Happy with Donald Trump's SCOTUS Shortlist," *CBS Local Philadelphia*, May 19, 2016.

CHAPTER 5

1. Emma Brown, "U.S. High School Seniors Slip in Math and Show No Improvement in Reading," *Washington Post*, April 27, 2016.

2. Donald J. Trump, *The America We Deserve* (Los Angeles: Renaissance Books, 2000).

3. Donald J. Trump, *Crippled America: How To Make America Great Again* (New York: Threshold, 2015).

4. Terence P. Jeffrey, "D.C. Schools: $29,349 Per Pupil, 83% Not proficient in Reading," CNS News, May 14, 2014.

5. Danielle Douglas-Gabriel, "Remedial Classes Have Become a Hidden Cost of College," *Washington Post*, April 6, 2016.

6. Donald J. Trump, *The America We Deserve* (Los Angeles: Renaissance Books, 2000).

7. Donald J. Trump, *Crippled America: How To Make America Great Again* (New York: Threshold, 2015).

8. Donald J. Trump, *The America We Deserve* (Los Angeles: Renaissance Books, 2000).

9. Donald J. Trump, *Crippled America: How To Make America Great Again* (New York: Threshold, 2015).

10. Ronald Reagan, "Remarks to Members of the National Governors' Association," *American Presidency Project*, February 22, 1988.

11. "The Federal Budget Fiscal Year 2012," White House, https://www.whitehouse.gov/omb/factsheet_department_education/.

12. "Education Department Budget History Table: FY 1980–FY 2016 President's Budget," U.S. Department of Education, February 8, 2016.

13. Donald J. Trump, *Crippled America: How To Make America Great Again* (New York: Threshold, 2015).

CHAPTER 6

1. Donald J. Trump, *Think Big: Make It Happen in Business and Life* (New York: Harper, 2007).

2. Donald J. Trump with Meredith McIver, *Trump — Never Give Up: How I Turned My Biggest Challenges Into Success* (Hoboken, NJ: Wiley, 2008).

3.   Donald J. Trump, *Time to Get Tough: Making America #1 Again* (Washington D.C.: Regnery Publishing, Inc., 2011).

4.   Donald J. Trump, *Trump 101: The Way to Success* (Wiley, 2009), 166.

5.   Donald J. Trump, *Crippled America: How to Make America #1 Again* (New York: Threshold, 2015).

6.   Donald J. Trump, *The America We Deserve* (Los Angeles: Renaissance Books, 2000).

7.   Susan Berry, "Dr. Meg Meeker: Trump's Relationship With His Daughter Ivanka Proves He's Not a Chauvinist," Breitbart News, May 10, 2016.

8.   Donald J. Trump, *Crippled America: How to Make America #1 Again* (New York: Threshold, 2015).

9.   George Beahm, *Trump Talk* (Adams Media, 2016).

10.   Samuel Smith, "Donald Trump 'Checks All the Boxes' on Abortion, Marriage, Religious Liberty, Ralph Reed Says," *Christian Post:* May 15, 2016.

11.   Michael Barbaro, "Trump on Abortion, Swear Words, and Handshakes," *New York Times*, May 3, 2011.

12.   Nina Bahadur, "Donald Trump Gets Womansplained On Planned Parenthood," *Huffington Post*, September 10, 2015.

13.   David Brody, "Donald Trump Comes Out in Support of 20-Week Abortion Ban," CBN News, April 2011.

14.   George Beahm, *Trump Talk* (Adams Media, 2016).

15.   Steven Ertelt, "Donald Trump: 'I Will Appoint Supreme Court Judges Who Will Be Pro-Life,'" LifeNews, May 11, 2016.

CHAPTER 7

1.   Donald J. Trump, *The America We Deserve* (Los Angeles: Renaissance, 2000).

2.   Ibid.

3.   Ibid.

4.   Robert D. Novak, "Cutting Government Down to Size: Will It Work?," *Imprimis*, April 1991.

5. Robert D. Novak, "A Senator's Railroad No-Brainer," *Washington Post*, March 5, 2007.

CHAPTER 8
1. Ronald Reagan, "Address to the Nation," White House, Washington, D.C., January 6, 1984.
2. Patrick Poole, "A Detailed Look at 'the Purge' of U.S. Counter-Terrorism Training by the Obama Administration," Blaze, March 26, 2014.
3. Lauren Walker, "TSA Investigation Finds 73 Workers on U.S.' Terrorist Watch List," *Newsweek*, June 10, 2015.
4. Jose Lambiet, Martin Gould, and Laura Collins, "FBI Investigating 'Conspiracy' Tip from a Rose Peddler Who Claims Orlando Shooter and His 'Pretty-Eyed' Wife Met Regularly with a Group of Six Other 'Foreigners' in a Dark Corner of a West Palm Beach Bar," *Daily Mail*, June 17, 2016.
5. Liz Sheld, Twitter post, June 18, 2016.
6. David Inserra, "Massacre in Orlando: 86th Instance of Islamist Terror in U.S. Since 9/11," Daily Signal, June 14, 2016.
7. Daniel Pipes, Twitter post, June 17, 2016, 12:36 p.m.
8. Jesse Byrnes, "Trump on Obama and Islam: 'There's Something Going On," *The Hill*, June 13, 2016.
9. Daniel Pipes, "Obama: 'My Muslim Faith,'" *Washington Times*, September 11, 2012.
10. Toby Harnden, "Barack Obama: NASA Must Try To Make Muslims 'Feel Good,'" *Telegraph*, July 6, 2016.
11. J. Taylor Rushing, "FBI Admits There's No Way to Screen All the Syrian Refugees the Obama Administration Plans to Accept Into the US," *Daily Mail*, October 21, 2015.
12. Ibid.
13. Caroline May, "Chart: Obama Admin. On Pace to Issue One Million Green Cards to Migrants from Majority-Muslim Countries," Breitbart News, June 17, 2016.

14.   Gary Detman, "Omar Mateen Had Behavioral Issues in School, Records Show," CBS12, June 16, 2016.

15.   Michael Goodwin, "Stop Blaming Orlando Shooting on Everything But Radical Islam," *New York Post*, June 13, 2016.

16.   Morgan Lee, "Why Are There Only 53 Christians Among America's 2,184 Syrian Refugees?," *Christianity Today*, November 20, 2015.

17.   Patrick Goodenough, "Record 499 Syrian Refugees Admitted to US So Far in May Includes No Christians," CNS News, May 23, 2016.

18.   Michael Patrick Leahy, "Politifact Says Trump Is Right: Hillary Clinton Supports '500% Increase in Syrian Refugees,'" Breitbart News, June 15, 2016.

19.   Donald J. Trump, Twitter post, June 12, 2016, 1:47 p.m.

20.   Mark Steyn, "A Great Statue, a Third-Rate Poem," *SteynOnline*, April 11, 2016.

21.   Tierney Sneed, "Paul Ryan on Stopping A President Trump's Muslim Ban: We'll Sue Him!," *Talking Points Memo*, June 17, 2016.

22.   Caroline May, "More Than 90 Percent of Middle Eastern Refugees on Food Stamps," Breitbart News, September 10, 2015.

23.   Jonah Bennett, "Like Father, Like Son: Orlando Terrorist's Father Expressed Support for Afghan Taliban," Daily Caller, June 12, 2016.

24.   Emily Schultheis, "Donald Trump Warns Refugees Could Be 'Trojan Horse' for U.S.," CBS News, June 13, 2016.

25.   Jim Tice, "Army Shrinks to Smallest Level Since Before World War II," *Army Times*, May 7, 2016.

26.   Donald J. Trump, "Donald J. Trump Foreign Policy Speech," TRUMP, April 27, 2016.

27.   Norman Leahy, "Nuke Forces Run Via Floppy Disks?!," *AMI Newswire*, May 26, 2016.

28.   "Full Transcript: POLITICO's Glenn Thrush interviews Sen. Jeff Sessions," *Politico*, May 31, 2016.

29. Ron Radosh, "Robert Kagan's Premature and Wrongheaded Decision to Endorse Clinton," *PJ Media*, February 27, 2016.

30. Edward Klein, *Unlikeable: The Problem with Hillary* (Washington, D.C.: Regnery, 2015).

31. Joseph S. Nye, Jr., *The Future of Power* (New York: PublicAffairs, 2011).

32. Reid Wilson, "Texas Officials Warn of Immigrants with Terrorist Ties Crossing Southern Border," *Washington Post*, February 28, 2015.

33. Larry O'Connor, "Report: Afghan and Pakistani Suspects Caught Crossing Mexican Border, Released by Obama Administration," *Hot Air*, June 3, 2016.

34. Caroline May, "Border Patrol Apprehends More than 33K Illegal Immigrants—1,075 per Day—in March," Breitbart News, April 22, 2016.

35. See www.usdebtclock.org. Accessed June 2016.

36. "U.S. Fiscal Year Budget Deficit Narrows to $439 Billion," Reuters, October 15, 2015.

37. "BLS: Americans Not in the Labor Force Soar to 94.7 Million," Newsmax, June 3, 2016.

38. Robert Schlesinger, "The Size of the U.S. and the World in 2016," *U.S. News and World Report*, January 5, 2016.

39. Daniel Wiser, "Report Finds That Shrinking Armed Forces Are Less Able to Respond to Global Threats," *Washington Free Beacon*, February 24, 2015.

40. "2015 Index of U.S. Military Strength," Heritage Foundation, 2015.

41. James S. Robbins, "Intervening in Syria Is Tough, But the Civilian Victims Deserve It," *U.S. News and World Report*, February 14, 2012.

42. "Worst Foreign Policy Ever," *Washington Times*, September 23, 2009.

43. Leo Shane III and George R. Altman, "Military Times Survey: Troops Prefer Trump to Clinton by a Huge Margin," *Military Times*, May 10, 2016.

CHAPTER 9

1. Donald J. Trump, *Crippled America: How to Make America #1 Again* (New York: Threshold: 2015).
2. Donald J. Trump, *The America We Deserve* (Los Angeles: Renaissance, 2000).
3. Todd Campbell, "It Would Be Dumb to Ignore These 5 Social Security Facts," *Motley Fool*, May 27, 2016.
4. George Beahm, *Trump Talk* (Adams Media, 2016).
5. Donald J. Trump, *Time to Get Tough: Making America #1 Again* (Regnery Publishing, Inc., 2011).
6. Donald J. Trump, *Crippled America: How to Make America #1 Again* (New York: Threshold: 2015).
7. Ibid.
8. Donald J. Trump, "Healthcare Reform to Make America Great Again," TRUMP, https://www.donaldjtrump.com/positions/healthcare-reform.
9. Donald J. Trump, *Crippled America: How to Make America Great Again* (New York: Threshold, 2015).
10. Curt Devine, "307,000 Vets May Have Died Awaiting VA Care, Report Says," CNN, September 3, 2015.
11. "Employment Situation of Veterans Summary," Bureau of Labor Statistics, March 22, 2016.
12. Charlie Spiering, "Records: Hillary Clinton Has Donated $70,000 to Veterans," Breitbart News, June 1, 2016.
13. Donald J. Trump, "Veterans Administration Reforms That Will Make America Great Again," TRUMP, https://www.donaldjtrump.com/positions/veterans-administration-reforms.
14. Donald J. Trump, *Time to Get Tough: Making America #1 Again*, (Regnery Publishing, Inc., 2011).

CHAPTER 10

1. Donald J. Trump, *Time to Get Tough: Making America #1 Again*, (Washington D.C.: Regnery Publishing, Inc., 2011).

2.   Ronald Reagan, "First Inaugural Address," *Governors'*
        Gallery, January 5, 1967.

CONCLUSION
1.   Donald J. Trump, *Crippled America: How to Make*
        America Great Again (New York: Threshold, 2015).
2.   Donald J. Trump, *The America We Deserve*, (Los
        Angeles: Renaissance, 2000).
3.   "Bush Ambassador to U.N. Drops Trump Bombshell,"
        Conservative Tribune, May 9, 2016.
4.   Phillip Jennings, "Would God Vote For Trump,"
        Breitbart News, June 14, 2016.

Index